# BASIC
## English Grammar
*for Speaking & Writing*

1권

## BASIC English Grammar
## for Speaking & Writing 1권

**2025년 01월 02일 인쇄**
**2025년 01월 10일 발행**

지 은 이  E & C
발 행 인  Chris Suh
발 행 처  **MENTORS**

경기도 성남시 분당구 황새울로 335번길 10 598
TEL 031-604-0025 FAX 031-696-5221
mentors.co.kr
blog.naver.com/mentorsbook
* Play 스토어 및 App 스토어에서 '멘토스북' 검색해 어플다운받기!

등록일자  2005년 7월 27일
등록번호  제 2009-000027호
I S B N  979-11-94467-20-5
979-11-94467-19-9(세트)
가    격  16,000원(정답 및 해설 PDF 무료다운로드)

# BASIC
# English
# Grammar

*for Speaking & Writing*

# 머리말

## ▶ 문법이란?

문법이란 문장을 만들어 말을 하고(speaking) 또한 문장을 만드는(writing) 것을 말한다. 모국어를 하는데는 그리 많은 문법이 필요하지 않는다. 어머니 뱃속에서부터 히어링을 하면서 모국어를 익히기 때문에 저절로 알게 되며 나중에 문법의 체계화를 위해 후천적으로 문법을 약간 학습할 뿐이다. 그러나 모국어가 아닌 외국어로 영어를 배우는 과정은 모국어 습득과 정반대가 된다.

## ▶ 외국어로 영어배우기는…

우리는 영어듣기와 영어말하기에 먼저 노출될 수 없기에 역으로 영문법을 통해서 영어를 말하고 쓰게 되는 과정을 밟아간다. 즉 한 언어, 즉 여기서는 영어를 문법을 통해서 이해하고 이를 발판으로 해서 영어회화, 영어작문 그리고 영어듣기 등에 많은 시간을 쏟고 주구장창 몰두하게 된다. 모국어로 영어를 배우는 네이티브와는 비교될 수 없는 싸움을 하는 것이다. 미국이나 영국에서 네이티브들과 소통하면서 몇년 살면 저절로 배워지는 영어지만 다 그럴 수 없기 때문에 우리는 어쩔 수 없이 비효율적인 방법으로 영어로 익힐 수밖에 없다. 여기에 문법의 중요성이 생기게 된다.

## ▶ 문법에만 흠뻑 빠지면 안돼…

여기서 한가지 범하기 쉬운 오류가 있다. 문법이 외국어를 배우는 최초의 단계임에는 분명하지만 너무 문법에 사로잡혀서 그래서 완벽한 문장 아니면 말을 하지 못하는 어리석음에 놓일 수가 있다. 언어는 시대에 따라 시시각각 변하고 이를 밑받침하는 문법 역시 계속 변화가 된다. 역으로 생각을 해보자. 우리가 특히 일상생활에서 우리말을 할 때 얼마나 국문법 규칙을 지키면서 말하는지 말이다. 이 말은 문법을 꼭 알아야 하지만 너무 문법에 얽매이면 안된다는 얘기이다.

## ▶ 이거 알면 남들보다 앞서가…

이 책 <BASIC English Grammar 1권, 2권>과 <SMART English Grammar 1권, 2권>은 지금 시대에 가장 잘 맞는 그리고 꼭 알아야 하는 문법규칙들을 무겁지 않게 정리하여 문법을 공부하는 사람들이 부담스럽지 않게 학습할 수 있도록 꾸며져 있다. 또한 이를 각종 Test들로 확인하게 되어 이를 다 풀고 나면 남들보다는 한두단계 영어에서 앞서 갈 수 있을 것이라 확신한다.

# New Grammar is About

## 1 실용영어를 위한 문법

문법도 실용영어를 하는데 필요한 최소한의 도구이다. 따라서 문법을 위한 문법이 아닌 '실용영어를 위한 문법' 이란 캐치프레이즈를 내걸고 실제로 영어를 읽고 말하는 데 필요한 영어문법 사항들만을 정리하였다. 가장 실용적인 영어회화문(Dialogue)을 통해 우리가 학습해야 할 문법사항을 언급하는 것 또한 '지금,' '현재' 쓰이고 있는 문법을 지향하기 위함이다.

## 2 영어회화를 위한 문법

실용영어의 목적은 영어로 하는 의사소통이다. '영어말하기' 란 목표를 달성하기 위해 문법에 영어회화를 접목해본다. 문법을 단순한 지식으로 책상에서만 필요한 것이 아니라 실제 영어로 말하는데 활용할 수 있도록 매 Unit별로 학습한 문법지식을 바탕으로 다양한 문장을 영어로 옮겨보는 훈련을 해보며 간접적인 영어회화훈련을 시도해본다. 이는 또한 점점 실용화되고 있는 영어시험자격증인 TOEFL, TOEIC, IELT 등에서 고득점을 취할 수 있는 기본 베이스가 될 수 있을 것이다.

## 3 다양한 테스트

학습한 문법사항은 연습을 통해 훈련하지 않으면 다 날아가버린다. 이런 과오를 범하지 않기 위해 각 Unit마다 다양한 연습문제를 그리고 각 Chapter가 끝날 때마다 Review Test를 통해 이중으로 테스트를 해보며 머리 속에 오래도록 각인해본다. '영어말하기' 뿐만 아니라 각종 시험에서도 높은 점수를 받을 수 있을 것이다.

# New Grammar is Organized

## 1 Chapter

문장의 기본개념으로부터 시작해서 문장의 종류, 동사, 시제, 부정사와 동명사, 분사, 수동태 등 총 8개의 Chapter로 실용영문법의 엑기스만을 집중 구분하여 정리하였다.

### 총 8개의 Chapters

Chapter 01 | 문장의 기본개념
Chapter 02 | 문장의 종류
Chapter 03 | 문장의 5형식
Chapter 04 | 동사
Chapter 05 | 시제
Chapter 06 | 부정사와 동명사
Chapter 07 | 분사
Chapter 08 | 수동태

## 2 Unit

Chapter는 다시 세분되어 각 Chapter별로 2~7개의 Unit로 정리된다. 따라서 총 8개의 Chapter는 총 38개의 Unit로 구성되어 있으며 각 Unit는 다시 Grammar in Practice, Grammar in Use, Unit Test, Writing Pattern Practice 등으로 나누어 진다.

### 각 Unit의 구성

Grammar in Practice
Grammar in Use
Unit Test
Writing Pattern Practice

## 3 Review

각 Chapter가 끝날 때마다 Chapter에서 학습한 내용을 다시 복습할 공간을 마련하였다. Review 1, 2에서 종합적으로 문제를 풀어보면서 자신이 학습한 내용을 얼마나 습득하였는지를 확인해볼 수 있다.

## 4 정답 및 해설

각 Unit의 테스트와 Review의 문제에 대한 정답을 별도의 부록을 처리하여 문제를 풀 때 정답에 접근하는 것을 어렵게 하여 가급적 스스로 풀어보도록 꾸며졌다.

# How to Use this Book

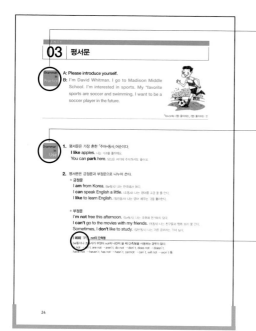

## Grammar in Practice
영어회화와 문법을 접목시키는 부분. 각 Unit에서 학습할 문법사항이 실제 영어회화에서는 어떻게 쓰이는지 보면서 문법을 왜 배워야 하는지를 느껴본다.

## Grammar in Use
역시 실용성에 focus를 맞춰 불필요한 문법지식을 다 걷어내고 오직 실제로 영어를 말하고 쓰는데 필요한 문법엑기스만을 간단하지만 밀도있게 서술하고 있는 부분이다.

## More Tips
Grammar in Use에서 못다한 추가정보를 그때그때마다 간략이 설명해준다.

## Unit Test
각 Unit마다 학습한 문법사항을 바로 확인해보는 자리이다. 다양한 형태의 테스트를 통해 학습한 문법지식을 머리 속에 차곡차곡 잊지 않고 기억해둘 수 있다.

## Writing Pattern Practice
이번에는 좀 더 적극적으로 문법과 영어회화를 접목시키는 공간이다. 학습한 문법사항을 실제로 영어말하는데 활용해 볼 수 있는 공간으로 문법이 살아있음을 느낄 수 있다.

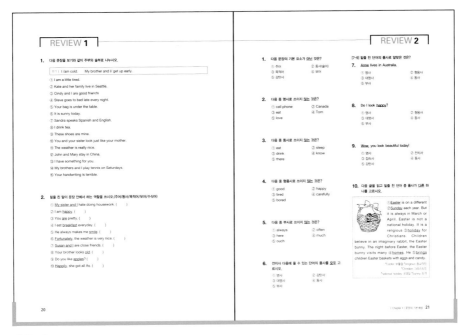

## Review

각 Chapter별로 제공되는 테스트시간으로 일종의 종합문제이다. 이미 Unit Test로 한번 확인한 문법을 다시
한번 꼭꼭 기억할 수 있는 공간이다.

## Wrap UP

군데군데 혼란스럽거나 복잡해보일 때마다 일목
요연하게 1페이지로 학습내용을 깔끔하게 정리하
였다.

# New Grammar Level 1-A
# Contents

### Chapter 01 | 문장의 기본개념
**Unit 1.** 문장의 구성      14
**Unit 2.** 단어의 종류      17

**Review 1**      20
**Review 2**      21

### Chapter 02 | 문장의 종류
**Unit 3.** 평서문      24
**Unit 4.** 명령문과 let's      27
**Unit 5.** 동사로 시작하는 의문문      30
**Unit 6.** 의문사로 시작하는 의문문 1      33
**Unit 7.** 의문사로 시작하는 의문문 2      37
**Unit 8.** 부정의문문과 부가의문문      40
**Unit 9.** 감탄문      43

**Review 1**      46
**Review 2**      47

### Chapter 03 | 문장의 5형식
**Unit 10.** 1, 2형식      50
**Unit 11.** 3형식      53
**Unit 12.** 4형식      56
**Unit 13.** 5형식      59

**Review 1**      62
**Review 2**      63

### Chapter 04 | 동사
**Unit 14.** Be동사      66
**Unit 15.** 일반동사      69
**Unit 16.** 조동사 can/could      72
**Unit 17.** 조동사 may/might      75
**Unit 18.** 조동사 will/would      78
**Unit 19.** 조동사 shall/should/had better      81
**Unit 20.** 조동사 must/have to/have got to      84

**Review 1**      88
**Review 2**      89

Chapter 05 | **시제**

**Unit 21.** 현재시제     92

**Unit 22.** 현재진행시제     95

**Unit 23.** 과거시제     98

**Unit 24.** 과거진행시제     102

**Unit 25.** 현재완료시제     105

**Unit 26.** 미래시제     108

**Review 1**     112

**Review 2**     113

Chapter 06 | **부정사와 동명사**

**Unit 27.** 명사 역할을 하는 to 부정사     116

**Unit 28.** 형용사 역할을 하는 to 부정사     119

**Unit 29.** 부사 역할을 하는 to 부정사     122

**Unit 30.** to 부정사의 의미상 주어     125

**Unit 31.** to 부정사를 이용한 다양한 표현     128

**Unit 32.** 동명사의 역할     131

**Unit 33.** 목적어로 쓰이는 부정사와 동명사     134

**Review 1**     137

**Review 2**     138

Chapter 07 | **분사**

**Unit 34.** 현재분사     140

**Unit 35.** 과거분사     143

**Unit 36.** 분사구문     146

**Review 1**     149

**Review 2**     150

Chapter 08 | **수동태**

**Unit 37** 능동태와 수동태     152

**Unit 38.** 수동태 표현     155

**Review 1**     158

**Review 2**     159

# *Chapter 1 | 문장의 기본개념

문장의 구성 | Unit 1
단어의 종류 | Unit 2

# 01 | 문장의 구성

**Grammar in Practice**

A: Happy birthday. I have something for you.
B: Thank you. Wow, what a beautiful hat!
A: Do you like it?
B: Yes, I really like it. Your gifts always make me happy.

**Grammar in Use**

**1.** 문장은 크게 주부(주어)와 서술부(동사, 목적어, 보어, 문장의 나머지)로 나눌 수 있다.

<u>My sister and I</u> <u>hate doing house work, especially dishwashing</u>.
　　　주부　　　　　　　　　　　서술부
언니와 나는 집안일 특히 설거지를 싫어한다.

**2.** 주어(subject, ～가)와 동사(verb, ～이다/～하다)가 주부와 서술부의 핵심이다.

**I am** happy. 나는 행복하다.
주어 동사

**My brother gets up** early. 남동생은 일찍 일어난다.
　　주어　　　　동사

**3.** 동작의 대상이 필요할 때는 목적어(object, ～을)를 쓴다. 명사/대명사가 목적어 역할을 한다.

I eat **breakfast** at 8:00. 나는 8시에 아침을 먹는다.
　　　목적어

**4.** 주어나 목적어에 대해 보충 설명하기 위해 보어(compliment)를 쓴다. 각각 주격보어와 목적격보어라고 말한다.

You look **pretty**. 너 예뻐 보인다.
　* you가 pretty하므로 pretty는 주격보어

He always makes me **happy**. 그는 나를 항상 행복하게 한다.
　　　　　　　　　* me가 happy하므로 happy는 목적격보어

**5.** 문장의 기본요소(주어, 동사, 목적어, 보어)를 설명하거나 수식해주는 수식어(modifier)가 있다. 형용사(구)와 부사(구)가 주로 수식어 역할을 한다.

Look at the girl **with blond hair**. 금발머리 여자애를 봐라.
　　　　　　　the girl을 수식하는 수식어이다

**Fortunately**, the weather is very nice. 다행히 날씨가 매우 좋다.
문장전체를 수식하는 수식어이다

# Unit Test

**1.** 문장에는 O를, 아닌 것에는 X를 쓰시오.

1. Pretty flowers (     )
2. She's my sister (     )
3. It a pen (     )
4. He likes apples (     )
5. raining heavily (     )

**2.** 다음 문장에서 주어를 찾아 동그라미 하시오.

1. I go to school.
2. Mary is my friend.
3. My parents are really nice.
4. The weather is not so good.
5. This bicycle was very expensive.

**3.** 지문을 읽고 동사가 몇 개인지 쓰시오. (     ) * 준동사 제외

I have a lot of friends in other countries.

Cindy Chow lives in Hong Kong. She takes Korean lessons at her school. Akiko lives in Japan. She studies at Kenzi Middle School. Lisa lives in the United States. She likes cooking and wants to be a cook in the future.

I miss them all.

**4.** 빈칸에 내용상 가장 알맞은 목적어를 보기에서 골라 쓰시오.

보기 |  the room    soccer    cereal    mathematics    Coke

1. I study _____ .
2. She wants to drink _____ .
3. Tom eats _____ for breakfast.
4. We play _____ after school.
5. They will clean _____ .

**5.** 밑줄 친 단어가 주격보어인지 목적격보어인지 쓰시오.

1. I am <u>sick</u>. (          )
2. My son makes me <u>happy</u>. (          )
3. They feel <u>wonderful</u>. (          )
4. Mary looks <u>tired</u>. (          )
5. Leave me <u>alone</u>. (          )

# Writing Pattern Practice

**1.** 「주어 + 동사」

나는 일한다. _____

남동생은 공부를 열심히 한다. _____

아버지는 담배 피신다. _____

우리는 많이 먹는다. (a lot) _____

그들은 매일 운동한다. (exercise) _____

**2.** 「주어 + 동사 + 목적어」

나는 매일 아침을 먹는다. (eat) _____

Susan은 영어공부를 열심히 한다. _____

우리는 영화를 좋아한다. (movies) _____

**3.** 「주어 + 동사 + 주격보어」, 「주어 + 동사 + 목적어 + 목적격보어」

나는 행복하다. _____

너 예뻐 보인다. _____

Mary는 피곤하다. (tired) _____

그 차는 비싸다. (expensive) _____

그는 나를 항상 행복하게 한다. _____

나를 Liz라고 불러. (call) _____

**4.** 「기본문장 + 수식어 (형용사(구), 부사(구)」

다행히 날씨가 매우 좋다. (very nice) _____

나는 6시에 일어난다. _____

가능한 모든 일을 시도해라. (possible) _____

금발머리 여자애를 봐라. (with blonde hair) _____

우리는 코트에서 테니스를 친다. (on the tennis courts)

_____

# 02 | 단어의 종류

**Grammar in Practice**

A: What do you like about Daniel?
B: Well...he has a good sense of humor and makes me laugh a lot.
A: What does he look like?
B: He's quite handsome.

**Grammar in Use**

**1.** 문장을 이루는 단어의 종류는 다음과 같다.

- **명사(Noun)** – 사람, 사물 등의 이름을 나타내는 말(cell phone, computer, BMW, Canada, Tom, love 등)
  **Anne** lives in **Canada**. Anne은 캐나다에 산다.

- **대명사(Pronoun)** – 명사를 대신해서 쓰는 말(I, he, they, this, that, it 등)
  You can turn off the television. I'm not watching **it**. 텔레비전 꺼도 돼. 안보고 있어.

- **동사(Verb)** – 움직임이나 상태를 나타내는 말(eat, sleep, drink, take, drive, have, know 등)
  **Take** an umbrella. 우산 가져가.

- **형용사(Adjective)** – 성질이나 상태를 나타내는 말(good, happy, tired, bored 등)
  I'm **tired**. I want to go home. 피곤해. 집에 가고 싶어.

- **부사(Adverb)** – 때, 장소, 정도 등을 나타내는 말(always, usually, yesterday, carefully, here, there, much, a lot, quickly 등)
  Please listen **carefully**. 잘 들어주세요.

- **전치사(Preposition)** – 명사, 대명사 앞에 와서 도와주는 말(to, at, in, on, about 등)
  I can give you a ride **to** school. 학교에 데려다 줄 수 있어.

- **접속사(Conjunction)** – 앞, 뒤의 말들을 연결해 주는 말(and, but, or, if, because 등)
  Say yes **or** no. Yes 인지 No 인지 대답해.

- **감탄사(Exclamation)** – 놀람, 기쁨 등의 느낌을 나타내는 말(wow, oh, ouch, oops 등)
  **Wow**, what a lovely day! 와, 날씨좋다!

# Unit Test

1. 밑줄 친 낱말의 품사를 말하시오.

   1. Look <u>at</u> the sky.
      (        )
   2. <u>Oh</u>, how happy I am!
      (        )
   3. What time does school <u>begin</u>?
      (        )
   4. This bag is mine <u>and</u> that one is yours.
      (        )
   5. There are some <u>big</u> trees in the yard.
      (        )
   6. We can't go skiing. There isn't any <u>snow</u>.
      (        )
   7. <u>Erica</u> is talking to a man.
      (        )
   8. I can't work. I'm <u>too</u> tired.
      (        )
   9. Paul often <u>wears</u> a black hat.
      (        )
   10. "Where are you?" "I'm <u>in</u> my room."
       (        )
   11. The beach was <u>beautiful</u>.
       (        )
   12. Take a look <u>at</u> this picture.
       (        )
   13. My <u>favorite</u> color is purple.
       (        )
   14. Mike <u>and</u> I are friends.
       (        )
   15. I have two puppies. I love <u>them</u> very much.
       (        )

2. 문장에서 주어는 밑줄치고 동사는 동그라미 하시오.

   1. I eat breakfast every day.
   2. Jane exercises in the morning.
   3. This bag is very heavy.
   4. You look pretty today.
   5. Tom and I go to the same middle school.
   6. David's family has four members.
   7. You have a beautiful smile.

18

# Writing Pattern Practice _주어가 3인칭단수(he, she, it) 현재형일 때는 일반동사에 –(e)s를 붙인다

1. **명사 – 주어/ 목적어/ 보어역할 (cell phone, computer, BMW, Canada, Tom, love 등)**

   Anne은 캐나다에 산다.(in Canada) _____

   나는 핸드폰을 가지고 있다.(cell phone) _____

   이것은 내 컴퓨터다. _____

2. **대명사 – 주어/ 목적어/ 보어역할 (I, he, they, this, that, it 등)**

   그는 나의 선생님이다. _____

   이것은 내 가방이다. _____

   그들은 나의 친구들이다. _____

3. **동사 – 술어역할 (eat, sleep, drink, take, drive, have, know 등)**

   나는 여자친구가 있다. _____

   그녀는 회사에 차 몰고 다닌다.(drive to work) _____

4. **형용사 – 보어역할/ 명사 수식 (good, happy, tired, bored 등)**

   나는 피곤하다. _____

   날씨가 좋다.(nice) _____

   좋은 시간 보내라.(good) _____

5. **부사 – 형용사/ 동사/ 다른 부사/ 문장전체 수식 (always, usually, yesterday, here, there, much, a lot, quickly, carefully 등)**

   잘 들어주세요.(Please~) _____

   Sally는 많이 먹는다.(a lot) _____

6. **전치사 – 전치사+명사/ 대명사 (to, at, in, on, about 등)**

   열쇠는 테이블 위에 있어.(The keys~) _____

   우리 그것에 대해 이야기 하자.(Let's) _____

7. **접속사 – 단어/구/절 연결 (and, but, or, if, because 등)**

   Jack은 젊지만 그는 똑똑하다. _____

   Yes 인지 No 인지 말해. _____

8. **감탄사 – 기쁨/ 놀람/ 아픔 표현 (wow, oh, ouch, oops 등)**

   와, 너 차 멋있다!(great) _____

   오, 너 감기 걸렸구나!(have a cold) _____

**1.** 다음 문장을 보기와 같이 주부와 술부로 나누시오.

> 보기 | I/ am cold.    My brother and I/ get up early.

① I am a little tired.

② Kate and her family live in Seattle.

③ Cindy and I are good friends.

④ Steve goes to bed late every night.

⑤ Your bag is under the table.

⑥ It is sunny today.

⑦ Sandra speaks Spanish and English.

⑧ I drink tea.

⑨ These shoes are mine.

⑩ You and your sister look just like your mother.

⑪ The weather is really nice.

⑫ John and Mary stay in China.

⑬ I have something for you.

⑭ My brothers and I play tennis on Saturdays.

⑮ Your handwriting is terrible.

**2.** 밑줄 친 말이 문장 안에서 하는 역할을 쓰시오.(주어/동사/목적어/보어/수식어)

① My sister and I hate doing housework. (        )

② I am happy. (        )

③ You are pretty. (        )

④ I eat breakfast everyday. (        )

⑤ He always makes me smile. (        )

⑥ Fortunately, the weather is very nice. (        )

⑦ Susan and I are close friends. (        )

⑧ Your brother looks old. (        )

⑨ Do you like apples? (        )

⑩ Happily, she got all As. (        )

**1.** 다음 중 문장의 기본 요소가 <u>아닌</u> 것은?

① 주어          ② 동사(술어)
③ 목적어       ④ 보어
⑤ 감탄사

**2.** 다음 중 명사로 쓰이지 <u>않는</u> 것은?

① cell phone    ② Canada
③ eat            ④ Tom
⑤ love

**3.** 다음 중 동사로 쓰이지 <u>않는</u> 것은?

① eat            ② sleep
③ drink        ④ know
⑤ there

**4.** 다음 중 형용사로 쓰이지 <u>않는</u> 것은?

① good        ② happy
③ tired        ④ carefully
⑤ bored

**5.** 다음 중 부사로 쓰이지 <u>않는</u> 것은?

① always      ② often
③ here         ④ much
⑤ ouch

**6.** 전치사 다음에 올 수 있는 단어의 품사를 모두 고르시오.

① 명사         ② 감탄사
③ 대명사      ④ 동사
⑤ 부사

[7–9] 밑줄 친 단어의 품사로 알맞은 것은?

**7.** <u>Anne</u> lives in Australia.

① 명사         ② 형용사
③ 대명사      ④ 동사
⑤ 부사

**8.** Do I look <u>happy</u>?

① 명사         ② 형용사
③ 대명사      ④ 동사
⑤ 부사

**9.** <u>Wow</u>, you look beautiful today!

① 명사         ② 전치사
③ 접속사      ④ 동사
⑤ 감탄사

**10.** 다음 글을 읽고 밑줄 친 단어 중 품사가 <u>다른</u> 하나를 고르시오.

①<u>Easter</u> is on a different ②<u>Sunday</u> each year. But it is always in March or April. Easter is not a national holiday. It is a religious ③<u>holiday</u> for Christians. Children believe in an imaginary rabbit, the Easter bunny. The night before Easter, the Easter bunny visits many ④<u>homes</u>. He ⑤<u>brings</u> children Easter baskets with eggs and candy.

*Easter 부활절 *religious 종교적인
*Christian 그리스도인
*national holiday 국경일 *bunny 토끼

# *Chapter 2 | 문장의 종류

평서문 | Unit 3

명령문과 let's | Unit 4

동사로 시작하는 의문문 | Unit 5

의문사로 시작하는 의문문 1 | Unit 6

의문사로 시작하는 의문문 2 | Unit 7

부정의문문과 부가의문문 | Unit 8

감탄문 | Unit 9

## Unit

# 03 | 평서문

**Grammar in Practice**

A: **Please introduce yourself.**

B: **I'm David Whitman. I go to Madison Middle School. I'm interested in sports. My \*favorite sports are soccer and swimming. I want to be a soccer player in the future.**

\*favorite (형) 좋아하는, (명) 좋아하는 것

**Grammar in Use**

**1.** 평서문은 가장 흔한 「주어+동사」 어순이다.

   **I like** apples. 나는 사과를 좋아해요.

   You can **park** here. 당신은 여기에 주차해도 좋아요.

**2.** 평서문은 긍정문과 부정문으로 나누어 쓴다.

● 긍정문

   I **am** from Korea. (Be동사) 나는 한국에서 왔다.

   I **can** speak English a little. (조동사) 나는 영어를 조금 할 줄 안다.

   I **like** to learn English. (일반동사) 나는 영어 배우는 것을 좋아한다.

● 부정문

   'be동사'와 '조동사'의 부정은 뒤에 not을 붙이면 된다. '일반동사'의 부정은 동사가 현재형이면서 주어가 3인칭단수(She/He/It)이면 does not을 쓰고 나머지는 do not을 쓴다.

| 주어 | be 동사의 부정 | 조동사의 부정 | 일반동사의 부정 |
|---|---|---|---|
| I | am not(='m not) | | do not(=don't) |
| You | are not(='re not/aren't) | cannot | do not(=don't) |
| She/He/It | is not(='s not/isn't) | (=can't) | does not(=doesn't) |
| We/You/They | are not(='re not/aren't) | | do not(=don't) |

   \*be동사나 조동사가 부정어 not과 나란히 쓸 때 단축형('re not, aren't 등)을 사용하는 경우가 많다.

   **I'm not** free this afternoon. (Be동사) 나는 오후에 한가하지 않다.

   **I can't** go to the movies with my friends. (조동사) 나는 친구들과 영화 보러 못 간다.

   Sometimes, I **don't** like to study. (일반동사) 나는 가끔 공부하는 것이 싫다.

# Unit Test

**1.** 평서문에 동그라미 하시오.

1. Do you speak English? (　　)
2. How are you doing? (　　)
3. Tom can't come to class because he's very sick. (　　)
4. What a wonderful day! (　　)
5. Smoking is not *allowed here. (　　)　　*allowcd 허락된
6. My sister can speak English very well. (　　)
7. It's cold in Alaska. (　　)

**2.** 평서문이 아닌 문장에 동그라미 하시오.

1. What do you do? (　　)
2. I don't like playing basketball. (　　)
3. Does Tom exercise every day? (　　)
4. How interesting! (　　)
5. My grandparents live in the United States. (　　)
6. Are you *mad at me? (　　)　　*mad 화난
7. It snows a lot in Wisconsin. (　　)

**3.** 보기에서 알맞은 말을 골라 빈칸에 써넣어 평서문을 만드시오.

| 보기 | I'm　　like　　can　　don't　　live　　She's　　have |
| --- |

1. _____ 16 years old.
   나는 16살이다.

2. Jane isn't at home now. _____ at work.
   Jane은 지금은 집에 없다. 직장에 있다.

3. I _____ ski.
   나는 스키를 탈줄 안다.

4. I _____ like eating.
   나는 먹는 것을 좋아하지 않는다.

5. We _____ in an apartment.
   우리는 아파트에 살아요.

6. You _____ beautiful eyes.
   너는 아름다운 눈을 가졌구나.

7. My grandparents _____ hiking.
   할아버지와 할머니는 하이킹을 좋아하신다.

# Writing Pattern Practice

● 긍정문

**1.** 「주어 + am/are/is ~」

나는 한국에서 왔다. _____

너 예쁘구나. _____

David는 미국에 있다. (in the States) _____

**2.** 「주어 + can/will/must + 동사원형」

나는 영어를 할 줄 안다.(speak) _____

눈이 올거야. (It~) _____

너는 좌석벨트를 매야한다. (fasten your seatbelt) _____

**3.** 「주어 + 일반동사─(e)s」

나는 영어 배우는 것을 좋아한다. (like to) _____

너는 일찍 일어나는구나. _____

아빠는 담배를 피신다. _____

● 부정문

**4.** 「주어 + am/are/is not ~」

나는 한가하지 않다. (free) _____

너는 뚱뚱하지 않다. (fat) _____

너의 여동생은 여기에 있지 않아. _____

**5.** 「주어 + can/will/should not + 동사원형」

나는 영화 보러 못 간다. (go to the movies) _____

비가 안 올 거야. (It~) _____

사람들은 음주운전을 해서는 안된다. (drink and drive) _____

**6.** 「주어 + don't/doesn't + 동사원형」

나는 가끔 공부하는 것이 싫다. (Sometimes, like to) _____

너는 운동을 하지 않는구나. _____

엄마는 일하지 않으신다. _____

# 04 | 명령문과 Let's

**Grammar in Practice**

A: Let's see a movie tonight.
B: That sounds good. Pick me up at six, will you?
A: Yes, I will. Let's not see a horror movie this time.
B: OK. Don't be late.

**Grammar in Use**

1. 명령문은 상대방에게 지시할 때나 일상생활에서 '~을 하세요' 정도의 느낌으로 쓴다. 동사원형으로 시작하고 공손히 말하기 위해서는 앞에 Please 또는 뒤에 ~, please를 붙인다.
   **Be** good. 착하게 행동해.
   **Come** in. 들어와요.
   Please **make** yourself comfortable. 편안히 계세요.
   **Help** yourself, please. 마음껏 드세요.

2. 부정명령문은 Don't 혹은 Never로 시작한다.
   **Don't** be late. 늦지 마.
   **Don't** do that again. 다시는 그러지마.
   **Never** give up. 절대 포기 하지 마.

3. 「Let's~」는 '~하자'라는 뜻이며 Let us가 축약된 형태로 다음에 동사원형이 온다.
   **Let's** go to school. 우리 학교가자.
   **Let's** see a movie. 우리 영화보자.
   **Let's** take a five-minute break. 우리 5분 쉬자.
   ( = **Let's** take a break for five minutes.)

4. 「Let's not ~」은 다음에 동사원형이 와서 '~하지말자' 라는 뜻으로 쓴다.
   **Let's not** skip that class. 우리 수업 빼먹지 말자.
   **Let's not** see a movie. 우리 영화 보지 말자.
   **Let's not** cheat. 우리 커닝하지 말자.

# Unit Test

**1.** 문장을 괄호안의 지시대로 바꿔 쓰시오.

1. You're happy.(명령문)                              → _____
2. You're quiet.(명령문)                              → _____
3. You have some more coffee.(명령문)                 → _____
4. You take care of my son. (명령문)                  → _____
5. You get up early. (명령문)                         → _____
6. You're late for school. (부정명령문)               → _____
7. You get in the car. (부정명령문)                   → _____
8. You play soccer after school (부정명령문)          → _____
9. You *stay up all night. (부정명령문)               → _____
10. You play computer games too much. (부정명령문)    → _____

*stay up all night 밤을 새우다

**2.** 문맥상 가장 알맞은 말에 동그라미 하시오.

1. We're hungry. (Let's/ Let's not) go out to eat.
2. That movie might be boring. (Let's/ Let's not) see it.
3. I'm tired now. (Let's/ Let's not) talk about it later.
4. It's cold outside. (Let's/ Let's not) just stay inside.
5. We have a test tomorrow. (Let's/ Let's not) watch too much TV .

**3.** 우리말과 일치하도록 괄호 안의 단어를 알맞게 배열하시오.

1. 좋은 여행해. (a/ have/ trip/ good) _____
2. 나를 기다려. (for/ me/ wait) _____
3. 늦지 마라. (be/ don't/ late) _____
4. 우리 영화보자 (a/ let's/ see/ movie) _____
5. 네 핸드폰 꺼라. (cell phone/ your /turn off) _____
6. 우리 나가지 말자. (not/ let's/ go out) _____
7. 우리 조심하자. (let's/ careful/ be) _____
8. 네 오빠를 귀찮게 굴지 마.(bother/ don't/ your brother) _____
9. 우리 조용히 하자. (be/ let's/ quiet) _____
10. 우리 결석하지 말자. (not/ let's/ absent/ be) _____

28

# Writing Pattern Practice

**1.** 「동사원형 + ~」 '…해라'

행복해라. _____

착하게 행동해.(good) _____

들어와. _____

이 음악 들어봐. _____

좋은 여행해.(good) _____

나를 기다려. _____

네 핸드폰 꺼라.(turn off) _____

마음껏 드세요.(~, please) _____

**2.** 「Don't(Never) + 동사원형 ~」 '…하지 마라'

늦지 마.(be) _____

미안해 하지 마.(be) _____

다시는 그러지마.(again) _____

아무 말도 하지 마.(say anything) _____

네 오빠를 귀찮게 굴지 마.(bother) _____

절대 포기하지 마.(Never~) _____

**3.** 「Let's + 동사원형 ~」 '…하자'

우리 학교가자. _____

우리 밖에 나가자. _____

우리 영어공부하자. _____

우리 영화보자.(a movie) _____

우리 저녁먹자. _____

우리 조심하자.(be) _____

우리 조용하자.(be) _____

**4.** 「Let's not + 동사원형 ~」 '…하지 말자'

우리 나가지 말자. _____

우리 결석하지 말자. _____

우리 영화 보지 말자. _____

우리 커닝하지 말자.(cheat) _____

우리 그것에 관해 지금 얘기하지 말자.(talk) _____

# 05 | 동사로 시작하는 의문문

**Grammar in Practice**

A: **Do** you cook every day?
B: Yes, I do.
A: **Are** you a good cook?
B: Yes, I am.
A: **Can** you make spaghetti?
B: Sure. I can.

**Grammar in Use**

**1.** be동사가 들어간 문장의 의문문은 그 be동사가 문장의 첫머리에 온다.

| Am | I | |
|---|---|---|
| Are | we/you/they | happy/ free/ tired...? |
| Is | he/she/it | |

I **am** late → **Am** I late? 내가 늦었다. → 내가 늦었어?
You **are** free. → **Are** you free? 너는 한가하다. → 너는 한가하니?
He **is** lost. → **Is** he lost? 그는 길을 잃었다. → 그는 길을 잃었니?

**2.** 조동사가 들어간 문장의 의문문은 그 조동사가 문장의 첫머리에 온다.

| Can | I/we/you/they he/she/it | swim/ ski/ cook...? |
|---|---|---|
| | | 동사원형 |

You **can** speak English well. → **Can** you speak English well?
너는 영어를 잘한다. → 너는 영어를 잘하니?

He **can** swim. → **Can** he swim? 그는 수영을 할 수 있다. → 그는 수영을 할 수 있니?

**3.** 일반동사가 들어간 문장의 의문문은 인칭과 시제에 맞는 do의 형태가 문장의 첫머리에 온다.

| Do | I/we/you/they | work/ live /eat...? |
|---|---|---|
| Does | he/she/it | 동사원형 |

You **have** a lot of money. 너는 돈이 많구나. →**Do** you **have** a lot of money? 너는 돈이 많니?

He **gets up** early. 그는 일찍 일어난다. →**Does** he **get up** early? 그는 일찍 일어나니?
They **go** to church every Sunday. 그들은 일요일마다 교회에 간다.
→ **Do** they **go** to church every Sunday? 그들은 일요일마다 교회에 가니?

**4.** 동사로 시작한 의문문에 대한 답은 대부분 Yes 또는 No로 시작한다.
"Am I late?" --- "**Yes**, you are." 내가 늦었어? – 응, 그래.
"Can you swim?" --- "**No**, I can't." 너는 수영할 줄 알아? – 아니, 못해.
"Does Chris work?" --- "**Yes**, he does." Chris는 일해? – 응, 그래.

# Unit Test

**1.** 평서문을 의문문으로 바꾸시오.

1. It is a nice coat. → _____
2. The movie is boring. → _____
3. Jin goes hiking every weekend. → _____
4. Tom and John live near here. → _____
5. They can make it on time. → _____

*make it on time 정각에 도착하다

**2.** 의문문을 평서문으로 바꾸시오.

1. Can you speak English? → _____
2. Is Mark interested in music? → _____
3. Is it cold outside? → _____
4. Do Mr. and Mrs. Smith live in Hawaii? → _____
5. Are they sorry for being late? → _____

**3.** 알맞은 말에 동그라미 하시오.

1. (Do/ Does) you speak English?
2. (Do/ Does) your sister go to school?
3. (Do/ Does) he want to be an actor?
4. (Do/ Does) your brothers speak Japanese well?
5. (Do/ Does) Tom and Jack live in Canada?

**4.** 상대방 가족에 관한 질문입니다. 보기와 같이 만들어 보시오.

| 보기 | (have a dog?) | Do you have a dog? |
| | (your dog/ cute?) | Is your dog cute? |

**Questions**

1. (have a sister?) _____
2. (your sister/ pretty?) _____
3. (your sister and you/ go to the same middle school?)

_____

4. (live with your parents?) _____
5. (your parents/ go to church?) _____
6. (your father/*strict?) _____
7. (your mother/ work?) _____

**Answers**

Yes, I have one sister.

Yes, she is.


Yes, we do.

Yes, I do.

Yes, they do.

Yes, a little.

No, she doesn't.

*strict:엄격한

# Writing Pattern Practice

**1.** 「Am/Are/Is + 주어 + 형용사/명사?」 '당신은 …인가요?'

내가 예쁘니? _____

내가 뚱뚱하니?(fat) _____

너는 한가하니? _____

너는 학생이니? _____

우리가 길을 잃었니?(lost) _____

우리가 늦었니? _____

그녀는 모델이니? _____

그는 변호사니?(a lawyer) _____

여기 춥니?(it) _____

이것은 네 가방이니? _____

그들은 간호사들이니? _____


**2.** 「Can + 주어 + 동사원형?」 '당신은 …할 수 있나요?'

너는 영어 말할 수 있니? _____

그는 수영할 수 있니? _____

Tom은 요리를 잘할 수 있니? _____

그들은 스키탈 수 있니?(ski) _____

그 아이들은 노래를 잘 할 수 있니? _____


**3.** 「Do/Does + 주어 + 동사원형?」 '당신은 …하나요?'

제가 당신을 아나요? _____

너는 매일 요리하니? _____

너는 돈이 많니?(a lot of) _____

그는 일찍 일어나니? _____

그녀는 아침을 먹니?(eat) _____

네 남동생은 영어를 좋아하니? _____

Jin은 주말마다 하이킹 가니?(go hiking) _____

그들은 일요일마다 교회에 가니? _____

Tom과 John은 근처에 사니?(near here) _____

# Unit
# 06 의문사로 시작하는 의문문 1

**Grammar in Practice**

A: What do you do?
B: I'm a teacher.
A: Where do you teach?
B: I teach at Minsun High School.
A: When do you *leave for work?
B: I leave for work at 7:30 in the morning.
A: How do you get to school?
B: I drive there.

* leave for ~를 향해서 떠나다

---

**Grammar in Use**

1. 의문사의 종류는 who(누구), what(무엇), which(어떤 것), when(언제), where(어디서), why(왜), how(어떻게) 등이다.

2. 의문사가 있는 의문문의 어순은 다음과 같다.
   - be동사가 있는 문장의 의문문 : 「의문사+be동사+주어…?」
     **Where** is Kate? Kate는 어디 있어?
     "**Who** is it?" "It's me." 누구세요? 나야.
   - 조동사가 있는 문장의 의문문 : 「의문사+조동사+주어+동사원형…?」
     **How** can I get to the airport? 어떻게 공항에 가지?
     **What** should I do? 어떻게 해야 하지?
   - 일반동사가 있는 문장의 의문문 : 「의문사+do/does+주어+동사원형…?」 또는 「의문사+동사…?」
     의문사자신이 주어인 경우
     **Who** do you live with?(who는 전치사 with의 목적어역할) 너는 누구와 사니?
     **Who** lives in this house?(who는 주어역할) 이 집에는 누가 사니?

3. 의문사로 시작하는 의문문은 구체적인 정보를 요구한다.
   "**What**'s your name?" "My name is **Sue**." 너는 이름이 뭐니? 내 이름은 Sue야.
   "**Where** do you live?" "I live in **Canada**." 너는 어디에 사니? 캐나다에 살아.
   "**Who** do you live with?" 너는 누구와 함께 사니?
   "I live with **my parents**." 부모님과 함께 살아.
   "**Why** do you study English?" 너는 왜 영어공부 하니?
   "I want **to have friends from other countries**." 외국친구들과 사귀고 싶어서.
   "**How** do you study English?" 너는 어떻게 영어공부 하니?
   "I **take a conversation class**." 회화수업을 들어.
   "**When** do you study English?" 너는 언제 영어공부 하니?
   "I study English **every morning**." 매일아침 영어공부 해.

# Unit Test

**1.** 의미상 알맞은 의문사에 동그라미 하시오.

1. (Who/ How) wants to eat ice cream?
2. (Who/ Where) do you work?
3. "(Where/ Why) is Jack from?" "He's from Hong Kong."
4. (How/ Who) can I get to the mall?
5. (When/ Why) can't Sue come to the meeting?

**2.** 틀린 곳을 찾아 고쳐 쓰시오.(현재시제)

1. Where David live?        →  _____
2. Why you late?            →  _____
3. What your favorite color? →  _____
4. Where you exercise?      →  _____
5. Who you live with?       →  _____

**3.** 질문에 알맞은 답을 골라 연결하시오.

1. What's your name?                              No, it doesn't.
2. Who wants to play the role of the princess?    I do.
3. Do I look pretty?                              Kathy Kim
4. Does it taste like pizza?                      Yes, you do.
5. Do your parents go to church?                  Yes, they do.

**4.** 보기를 참고하여 주어진 답을 보고 의문문을 완성하시오.

> 보기 | A: <u>Why</u> <u>do</u> you want to go so early?
> B: Because I have to do something at home.

1. A: _____ _____ you live?
   B: I live in Singapore.
2. A: _____ _____ he get up?
   B: He gets up at 8:00 am.
3. A: _____ _____ you like?
   B: I like Susan very much.
4. A: _____ _____ Tom go to school?
   B: He takes a bus.
5. A: _____ _____ you eat for breakfast?
   B: We eat cereal for breakfast.

# Writing Pattern Practice

**1.** 「What ~?」 '무엇이/무엇을 …?'

> 「What+be동사+주어~?」
> 「What+do/does/조동사+주어+동사원형~?」
> 「What+동사~?」

너의 이름이 뭐야? _____

너는 좋아하는 색깔이 뭐니? _____

제가 무엇을 할 수 있을까요? _____

너는 아침식사로 뭐 먹니?(for breakfast) _____

Julie라는 사람 어떻게 생겼어?(look like) _____

Jack과 Molly는 무엇을 공부하니? _____

내가 어떻게 해야 하지?(What should~) _____

무엇이 너를 괴롭히니?(bother) _____


**2.** 「Where~?」 '어디에서 …?'

> 「Where+be동사+주어~?」
> 「Where+do/does/조동사+주어+동사원형~?」

너는 어디에 있니? _____

나는 어디에 있니?(=여기가 어디니?) _____

내 코트가 어디에 있지? _____

너는 어디에 사니? _____

David은 어디에서 운동하니? _____

그들은 어디서 파티를 하니? _____


**3.** 「Who ~?」 '누가/누구를 …?'

> 「Who+be동사+주어~?」
> 「Who+do/does/조동사+주어+동사원형~?」
> 「Who+동사~?」

누가 너의 친구니? _____

너는 누구를 좋아하니? _____

너는 누구와 함께 사니? _____

Jack은 누구를 사랑하니? _____

그들은 누구를 그리워하니? _____

누가 초콜릿을 좋아하지? _____

누가 그의 전화번호 아니? _____

누가 돈을 많이 가지고 있니?(a lot of) _____

**4.** 「Why ~?」 왜 …?

```
「Why+be동사+주어~?」
「Why+do/does/조동사+주어+동사원형~?」
```

너는 왜 화가 났니?(angry) _____

그들은 왜 결석했니? _____

너는 왜 영어공부 하니? _____

John은 왜 일찍 일어나니? _____

너의 삼촌은 왜 뉴욕에 사시니? _____

그들은 왜 그렇게 열심히 일하니?(so hard) _____


**5.** 「How ~?」 ~가 어때? 어떻게 …?

```
「How+be동사+주어~?」
「How+do/does/조동사+주어+동사원형~?」
```

너는 어떠니? _____

내가 거기에 어떻게 가죠?(get) _____

나 어때 보이니? _____

너는 어떻게 영어공부 하니? _____

그거 맛이 어떠니?(taste) _____

Tom은 학교에 어떻게 가니?(get) _____


**6.** 「When ~?」 언제 …?

```
「When+be동사+주어~?」
「When+do/does/조동사+주어+동사원형~?」
```

너는 생일이 언제니? _____

너는 언제 영어공부 하니? _____

Mary는 언제 저녁을 먹니? _____

언제 영화가 시작하니?(begin) _____

그들은 언제 회의를 하죠? _____

# 07 | 의문사로 시작하는 의문문 2

**Grammar in Practice**

A: What is your favorite holiday?
B: Thanksgiving.
A: Why do you like Thanksgiving best?
B: Because I can eat a delicious turkey dinner.

**Grammar in Use**

**1.** 의문사는 문장 안에서의 기능에 따라 의문대명사, 의문부사, 의문형용사로 나눌 수 있다.

**2.** 의문대명사 who, what, which는 주어 또는 목적어 역할을 한다.
**Who** likes you? (주어) 누가 너를 좋아해?
**Who** do you like? (목적어) 너는 누구를 좋아해?
**What** bothers you? (주어) 무엇이 너를 괴롭히니?
**What** do you eat for dinner? (목적어) 너는 저녁으로 무엇을 먹니?
**Which** is your bag? (주어) 어느 게 네 가방이니?
**Which** do you want to buy? (목적어) 너는 어느 것을 사고 싶니?

**3.** 의문부사 how, when, where, why 다음에 의문문 어순을 쓴다.
**How** are things going? 어떻게 지내니?
**How** do you like your new computer? 새로 산 컴퓨터 어때?
**When** is your birthday? 생일이 언제야?
**When** do they get off work? 그들은 언제 퇴근해?
**Where** is the bus stop? 버스정류장이 어디지?
**Where** does the bus stop? 그 버스 어디에 서?
**Why** are you so tired? 왜 그렇게 피곤한거야?
**Why** do you get up so early? 왜 그렇게 일찍 일어나니?

**4.** 의문형용사 what, which 다음에 항상 명사를 쓴다.
**What** bus do you take to get home? 집에 가려면 무슨 버스 타니?
**What** day is it today? 오늘이 무슨 요일이야?
**Which** bag is more expensive? 어느 가방이 더 비싸?

# Unit Test

**1.** 밑줄 친 의문사가 주어역할을 하는지 목적어 역할을 하는지 구분하여 쓰시오.

1. <u>Who</u> likes chocolate? (        )
2. <u>Who</u> do you want to invite? (        )
3. <u>What</u> bothers you? (        )
4. <u>What</u> do you want for Christmas? (        )
5. <u>Who</u> do you study with? (        )

**2.** who를 이용하여 보기와 같이 의문문 문장을 만드시오.

> 보기 | I want some cake. → <u>Who wants some cake?</u> (who : 주어 역할)

1. I have a lot of money.          → _____
2. I'm late for school.           → _____
3. Mr. Kim isn't at work.          → _____
4. Sue goes to bed early.          → _____
5. Angela doesn't like shopping.   → _____

**3.** what을 이용하여 보기와 같이 의문문 문장을 만드시오.

> 보기 | I want some grapes. → <u>What do I want?</u> (what : 목적어 역할)

1. You have some money.            → _____
2. Mary likes windsurfing.         → _____
3. Jane needs a bag.               → _____
4. I enjoy dancing.                → _____
5. Jack and Liz eat cereal for breakfast. → _____

**4.** 우리말과 일치하도록 괄호 안의 단어를 알맞게 배열하시오.

1. 공중전화는 어디에 있나요? (the/ is/ phone booth/ where/ ?)

   _____

2. 당신은 무슨 색을 가장 좋아해요? (what/ you/ color/ like/ do/ best/ ?)

   _____

3. 왜 당신은 늦었어요? (you/ are/ why/ late/ ?)

   _____

4. Mary는 언제 잠자리에 들죠? (does/ when/ Mary/ go to bed/ ?)

   _____

5. 당신 아버지는 어떻게 지내세요? (is/ your father/ how/ ?)

   _____

6. 어떤 의사선생님을 보길 원해요? (doctor/ do/ want/ which/ you/ to see/ ?)

   _____

# Writing Pattern Practice _일반동사가 들어간 문장의 의문문일 경우

**1.** 「Who + 동사 ~?」 '누가 …해요?' who-주어역할

누가 너를 좋아해? _____

누가 아이스크림 먹을래?(want) _____

누가 그 파티에 올거니?(will) _____

**2.** 「Who + do/does + 주어 + 동사원형 ~?」 '누구를 …해요?' who-목적어역할

너는 누구를 좋아해? _____

그녀는 누구를 초대하고 싶어해?(invite) _____

**3.** 「What + 동사 ~?」 '무엇이 …해요?' what-주어역할

무엇이 너를 괴롭히니? _____

무엇이 그를 피곤하게 만드니? _____

**4.** 「What + do/does + 주어 + 동사원형 ~?」 '무엇을 …해요?' what-목적어역할

너는 저녁으로 무엇을 먹니?(for dinner) _____

그것은 무엇을 의미하니?(mean) _____

그녀는 Christmas에 무엇을 원하니? _____

**5.** 「Which + 동사 ~?」 '어느 것이 …해요?' which-주어역할

어느 것이 주머니가 있나요?(a pocket) _____

**6.** 「Which + do/does + 주어 + 동사원형 ~?」 '어느 것을 …해요?' which-목적어역할

너는 어느 것을 사고 싶니?(want to buy) _____

그는 어느 것을 더 좋아하니?(prefer) _____

**7.** 「How, When, Where, Why + do/does + 주어 + 동사원형 ~?」 '어떻게, 언제, 어디서, 왜 …해요?'

너는 왜 그렇게 일찍 일어나니? _____

그들은 언제 퇴근해?(get off work) _____

**8.** 「What, Which + 명사 + do/does + 주어 + 동사원형 ~?」 '무슨/어떤 ~을 …하니?'

당신은 무슨 요일에 회의를 하죠? _____

어느 색깔이 더 좋으니, 분홍이니 보라니?(prefer) _____

# Unit

# 08 | 부정의문문과 부가의문문

Grammar in Practice

A: Look at that girl. Isn't she pretty?

B: Yes, she is. She is my type.

A: I think she goes to the same school as you, doesn't she?

B: I guess so.

Grammar in Use

**1.** 부정의문문이란 부정어가 들어간 의문문을 말하며 '~하지 않나요?' 로 해석한다. 대답하는 문장이 긍정문이면 yes, 부정문이면 no를 쓴다.

**Don't** you like music? 너는 음악을 좋아하지 않니?

Yes, I do. 아니, 좋아해. No, I don't. 응, 좋아하지 않아.

**2.** 부정의문문에서는 동사와 부정어를 축약된 형태로 문장 맨 앞에 쓴다.

**Aren't** you bored? 너는 지루하지 않니?

**Can't** you stay a little longer? 너는 조금만 더 있다 가면 안돼?

**Doesn't** your father smoke? 아버지가 담배피시지 않니?

**3.** 부가의문문이란 평서문으로 말하다가 상대방의 동의를 얻기 위해 뒤에 질문을 덧붙이는 형태를 말한다. 이때 덧붙여주는 문장은 앞의 문장이 긍정이면 부정, 부정이면 긍정으로 쓴다.

● 덧붙여지는 문장은 be동사나 조동사일 경우 그대로 사용한다.

You are sick, **aren't** you? 너 아프지, 그렇지 않니?

Mary isn't at home, **is** she? Mary는 집에 없지, 그렇지?

You can come to my birthday party, **can't** you? 너는 내 생일파티에 올 수 있지, 그렇지 않니?

He can't make spaghetti, **can** he? 그는 스파게티 못 만들지, 그렇지?

This is your muffler, **isn't** it? 이것은 네 목도리지, 그렇지 않니?

These dishes aren't clean, **are** they? 이 그릇들은 깨끗하지 않지, 그렇지?

**I MORE TIPS I** 앞문장의 this/ that 또는 these/those는 덧붙이는 문장에서 각각 it, they로 쓴다.

● 일반동사일 경우 do 조동사를 인칭과 시제에 맞게 사용한다.

You usually skip breakfast, **don't** you? 너는 보통 아침 안 먹지, 그렇지 않니?

Anna doesn't like math, **does** she? Anna는 수학을 좋아하지 않지. 그렇지?

They have an important meeting tomorrow, **don't** they?

그들은 내일 중요한 회의 있지, 그렇지 않니?

# Unit Test

**1.** 의문문을 부정의문문으로 바꾸시오.

1. Can you swim? → _____
2. Does Harry like hiking? → _____
3. Is this your hat? → _____
4. Is he your roommate? → _____
5. Are Paul and Jack close friends? → _____

**2.** 평서문을 부정의문문으로 바꾸시오.

1. He is a good swimmer. → _____
2. Women like shopping. → _____
3. You can park here. → _____
4. They live in that apartment. → _____
5. His parents enjoy hiking. → _____

**3.** 빈칸에 알맞은 말을 넣어 부가의문문 문장을 완성하시오.

1. Jack lives in Los Angeles, _____ _____ ?
2. You can's swim, _____ _____ ?
3. Gary and you are friends, _____ _____ ?
4. It doesn't snow in Hong Kong, _____ _____ ?
5. These flowers are so beautiful, _____ _____ ?

**4.** 우리말과 일치하도록 괄호 안의 단어를 알맞게 배열하시오.

1. 너 피곤하지 않니? (you/ aren't/ tired/ ?)

_____

2. 너의 남자친구는 Florida에 살지 않니? (doesn't/ in Florida/ your boyfriend/ live/ ?)

_____

3. Nicole이 New York 출신 아니니? (Nicole/ isn't/ from New York/ ?)

_____

4. Jack은 수업에 늦지 않았니? (for class/ Jack/ isn't/ late/ ?)

_____

5. 나 좀 더 자면 안 돼? (I/ can't/ sleep/ a little longer/ ?)

_____

# Writing Pattern Practice _주어가 2인칭 you가 아닐 때 주의!

**1.** 「Aren't you ~?」 '너는 …이지 않니?'

너 지루하지 않니? _____

그가 네 룸메이트 아니니? _____

날씨가 좋지 않니?(nice) _____

Nicole과 너는 New York 출신이 아니니? _____


**2.** 「Can't you ~?」 '너는 …할 수 있지 않니?'

내가 니책 빌리면 안 될까?(borrow) _____

너 조금 더 있다 가면 안 되니?(a little longer) _____

그는 우리 태워줄 수 없을까?(give us a ride) _____

우리 그것에 대해서 다음에 얘기하면 안 될까요? _____


**3.** 「Don't you ~?」 '너는 …하지 않니?'

너는 일찍 일어나지 않니? _____

아버지가 담배피시지 않니? _____

Sally는 일하지 않니? _____

그들은 음악을 좋아하지 않니? _____


**4.** 「You're/ aren't ~ , aren't/are you?」 '너는 …이지(이지 않지), 그렇지 않니(그렇지)?'

너 아프지, 그렇지 않니? _____

날씨가 좋다, 그렇지 않니? _____

Mary는 집에 없지, 그렇지?(at home) _____

Gary와 너는 친구지, 그렇지 않니? _____


**5.** 「You can/can't ~ , can't/can you?」 너는 …할 수 있지(없지), 그렇지 않니(그렇지)?

너 내 생일파티에 올 수 있지, 그렇지 않니? _____

Jane은 여기에 정각에 못 오지, 그렇지?(be here) _____

Tom과 네가 내 옆에 있어 줄 수 있지, 그렇지 않니? _____


**6.** 「You 동사/don't+동사 ~ , do/don't you?」 너는 …하지(하지 않지), 그렇지 않니(그렇지)?

너 축구하는 거 좋아하지, 그렇지 않니?(playing) _____

Mary는 수학을 안 좋아하지, 그렇지? _____

그들은 교복을 입지, 그렇지 않니?(school uniforms) _____

# Unit

# 09 | 감탄문

Grammar in Practice

A: What a great bike!
B: My uncle bought it for me.
A: Let's go for a bike ride tomorrow.
B: That would be nice!

Grammar in Use

**1.** 놀라움이나 감정을 강조하고 싶을 때 감탄문을 쓴다.
**How** exciting (it is)! 얼마나 흥미진진한지!
**What** pretty flowers (they are)! 꽃들이 얼마나 아름다운지!

**2.** How로 시작하는 감탄문은 다음에 형용사나 부사를 쓴다.
- 「How+형용사+주어+동사!」
**How** beautiful you are! 당신이 얼마나 아름다운지!
**How** exciting the game is! 그 게임이 얼마나 흥미진진한지!
- 「How+부사+주어+동사!」
**How** fast she ran! 그녀가 얼마나 빨리 뛰던지!
**How** wonderfully they sang! 그들이 얼마나 멋지게 노래하던지!

**3.** What으로 시작하는 감탄문은 다음에 명사를 쓴다.
- 「What+(a/an)+형용사+명사+주어+동사!」
**What** a great car you have! 정말 멋진 차를 가지고 있구나!
**What** great students you are! 너희들이 얼마나 멋진 학생들인지!
- 「What+(a/an)+명사+ 주어+ 동사!」 *형용사 없이 억양이나 표정으로 느낌을 대신할 수 있다.
**What** a day it is! 대단한(힘든/재수없는/멋진…) 날이군!
**What** a woman she is! 대단한(이상한/멋진…) 여자야!

**4.** 감탄문에서 주어, 동사는 특별한 뜻이 없을 때 생략하는 경우가 많다.
**How** beautiful! 얼마나 아름다운지!
**How** fast! 얼마나 빠른지!
**What** a great car! 정말 멋진 차군!
**What** a surprise! 정말 놀랍군!

# Unit Test

**1.** 빈칸에 What이나 How를 쓰시오.

1. _____ a great idea!
2. _____ nice it is!
3. _____ exciting!
4. _____ nice shoes!
5. _____ fast she ran!
6. _____ a day!
7. _____ a nice bike you have!
8. _____ happy I am!
9. _____ a wonderful world!
10. _____ beautiful Cindy is!

**2.** 문장을 감탄문으로 바꾸시오.

1. It is a very touching movie.
   → What _____ it is!
2. She is a very pretty girl!
   → What _____ she is!
3. They are very beautiful flowers.
   → What _____ they are!
4. The baby is very cute!
   → How _____ the baby is!
5. This book is very interesting.
   → How _____ this book is!

**3.** 우리말과 일치하도록 괄호 안의 단어를 알맞게 배열하시오.

1. 세상 참 좁군! (a/ what/ small/ world/ !)

   _____

2. 날씨 참 좋다! (day/ what/ a/ beautiful/ !)

   _____

3. 그 아기가 얼마나 사랑스러운지! (lovely/ how/ is/ the baby/ !)

   _____

4. 참 안됐다! (pity/ a/ what/ !)

   _____

5. 그가 얼마나 친절한지! (he/ kind/ how/ is/ !)

   _____

6. 정말 긴 하루다! (a/ what/ day/ long/ !)

   _____

7. 정말 멋있는 신발이다! (nice/ what/ shoes/ !)

   _____

44

# Writing Pattern Practice

**1.** 「How + 형용사 (+ 주어 + 동사!)」 '얼마나 …한지!'

당신이 얼마나 아름다운지! _____

그 게임이 얼마나 흥미진진한지!(exciting) _____

그 영화가 얼마나 지루했던지!(boring) _____

그가 얼마나 친절한지! _____

그 모델들이 얼마나 키가 큰지! _____

**2.** 「How + 부사 (+ 주어 + 동사!)」 '얼마나 …한지!'

그녀가 얼마나 빨리 뛰던지! _____

그들이 얼마나 멋지게 노래하던지!(wonderfully) _____

**3.** 「What + (a/an) + 형용사 + 명사 (+ 주어 + 동사!)」 '얼마나 …한지!'

정말 멋진 자전거네!(great) _____

정말 예쁜 꽃들이네! _____

너는 정말 멋진 차를 가지고 있구나!(great) _____

그 자전거가 얼마나 멋진지!(nice) _____

너희들이 얼마나 멋진 학생들인지!(great) _____

그 차들이 얼마나 비싼지!(expensive) _____

세상 참 좁군! _____

날씨 참 좋다!(beautiful day) _____

**4.** 「What + (a/an) + 명사!」 '얼마나 …한지!'

정말 놀라운데! _____

창피한 일이군!(a shame) _____

멋진 플레이야! _____

대단한 날이군! _____

참 안됐다!(a pity) _____

# REVIEW 1

**1.** 틀린 곳을 바르게 고치시오.

① Never gives up. → _____

② Let's not sees this movie. → _____

③ Don't being late. → _____

④ Do your sister go to the same school as you? → _____

⑤ Can he swims? → _____

⑥ Do she do her homework every day? → _____

⑦ Who eat breakfast every day? → _____

⑧ Doesn't the movie starts at 11:00? → _____

⑨ Where my backpack is? → _____

⑩ How does Tom goes to school? → _____

**2.** 다음 문장을 영어로 쓰시오.

① 우리 늦지 말자. → _____

② 그들은 어디에서 파티를 할거니?(will) → _____

③ 그 영화 어땠어? → _____

④ 너는 매일 숙제하지 않니? → _____

⑤ Jack은 수영할 수 있지, 그렇지 않니? → _____

**3.** 다음 문장을 우리말로 쓰시오.

① Doesn't it smell good? → _____

② Who wants to stay with Charlie? → _____

③ Your parents live in Busan, don't they? → _____

④ What a beautiful skirt it is! → _____

⑤ How boring this movie was! → _____

**4.** 문장을 괄호안의 지시대로 바꾸시오.

① I am late for work. (의문문으로) → _____

② Janet is raising two kittens.(의문문으로) → _____

③ Do you stay up late? (부정의문문으로) → _____

④ Does he practice English every day? (평서문으로) → _____

⑤ You have very beautiful hair. (What~ 감탄문으로) → _____

⑥ The concert was very exciting. (How~ 감탄문으로) → _____

⑦ You brush your teeth. (명령문으로) → _____

⑧ You don't drink too much. (명령문으로) → _____

**1.** 평서문을 고르시오.

① What a wonderful world!
② Do you get up early?
③ Go straight for three blocks.
④ Elizabeth lives in Chicago.
⑤ What do you do for a living?

**2.** 어법상 맞는 문장을 고르시오.

① Don't late!
② Let's not going there.
③ How can I getting to the airport?
④ Does your brother study hard?
⑤ Do she know the truth?

**3.** 문장 안에서 what이 할 수 있는 역할을 1개 이상 고르시오.

① 대명사      ② 형용사
③ 접속사      ④ 동사
⑤ 전치사

**4.** 보기의 who와 역할이 같은 것은?

> 보기 | Who likes apples?

① Who do you have lunch with?
② Who wants to drink some Coke?
③ Who does Jack like?
④ Who do you call every day?
⑤ Who does Jane talk to?

**5.** 다음 부정의문문 중 어법상 어긋난 것은?

① Can't I sleep a little longer?
② Don't you like English?
③ Aren't you tired?
④ Isn't they hungry?
⑤ Don't I look pretty?

**6.** 다음 부가의문문 중 보기의 문장을 넣으면 가장 알맞은 것은?

> 보기 | does she?

① She is at home, _____
② Susie isn't tired now, _____
③ Kelly doesn't live in Tokyo, _____
④ Your sister gets up early, _____
⑤ Terry and Tom don't study in Canada.
_____

**7.** 다음 글을 읽고 괄호안의 단어 중 알맞은 것을 골라 동그라미 하시오.

The Great Wall

Many people in China walk on the Great Wall. But don't ever (try/trying) to walk the distance of the whole thing. It's too long. (Do/Does) you (know/knows) its length? Imagine walking 4,000km from Los Angeles to New York. The Great Wall is a lot longer than that. It's more than 6,000 km long!

※ **Chapter 3** | **문장의 5형식**

1, 2형식 | Unit 10
3형식 | Unit 11
4형식 | Unit 12
5형식 | Unit 13

# Unit

# 10 | 1형식 2형식

Grammar
in
Practice

A: How do I look?

B: You look different today. You got a haircut, didn't you?

A: Yes, I did.

B: You look much younger than before.

Grammar
in
Use

**1.** 1형식문장은 주어와 동사만으로도 완전한 의미의 문장을 만들 수 있는 경우를 말한다. 부사나 부사구, 의문문, 부정문은 형식에 영향을 미치지 않는다.

I exercise. (1형식)   Do you exercise? (1형식)   I don't exercise. (1형식)

I exercise at the gym every morning. (1형식)

**2.** 1형식문장은 「주어+동사」의 형태로 '~가 …하다', '~가 있다' 등의 뜻을 갖는다.

Jane works. Jane은 일한다.

There are a lot of people here. 여기 사람들이 많다.

**3.** 2형식 문장은 「주어+동사+보어」의 형태로 보어가 주어의 상황을 보충 설명해준다. 이 때 명사와 형용사 등이 보어 역할을 한다.

Lisa became a doctor. Lisa는 의사선생님이 되었다.

You look very tired. 너 매우 피곤해 보인다.

**4.** 2형식에 주로 많이 쓰이는 동사는 다음과 같다.

● be동사

I **am** tall. 나는 키가 크다.

Susan **is** very embarrassed. Susan은 매우 당황했다.

● 감각동사 (look, smell, taste, sound, feel, seem 등)

You **look** different today. 너 오늘 달라 보인다.

Something **smells** bad. 뭔가 냄새가 나쁘다.

Does it **taste** good? 그거 맛있니?

"Let's eat out." "That **sounds** great." 외식하자. 좋아.

This fur coat **feels** soft. 그 털 코트는 촉감이 좋다.

This bag **seems** expensive. 그 가방이 비싼 듯하다.

● 변화동사 (become, get, turn, grow 등)

I'll **become** a doctor. 나는 의사가 될 거야.

Laura **got** bored. Laura는 지루해졌다.

The leaves **turned** red. 잎이 빨갛게 물들었다.

It **grew** dark. 어두워졌다.

# Unit Test

**1.** 다음 문장의 형식을 쓰시오.

> 「주어+동사」 → 1형식 「주어+동사+보어」 → 2형식

1. She exercises every day. (      )
2. Are you leaving soon? (      )
3. I don't care. (      )
4. You look bored. (      )
5. We are hungry. (      )
6. This soup tastes good. (      )
7. My father works. (      )
8. There are a lot of people here. (      )
9. I work on Saturdays. (      )
10. Are you feeling OK? (      )

**2.** 다음 단어 중 2형식에 주로 쓰이는 동사를 골라 ✓표 하시오.

| | | | | |
|---|---|---|---|---|
| become | play | want | hope | arrive |
| rain | snow | talk | be | sound |
| sing | sleep | study | feel | eat |

**3.** 우리말과 일치하도록 괄호 안의 단어를 알맞게 배열하시오.

1. 나는 매일 운동한다. (exercise/ I/ every day)
2. 너는 피곤해 보인다. (look/ you/ tired)
3. 나는 선생님이 될 거야. (become/ I'll/ a teacher)
4. 주스는 냉장고에 있어. (is/ the juice/in the fridge)
5. 나는 어제 밤 파티에 있었어요. (was/ I/ last night/ at the party)
6. 아버지는 담배를 많이 피신다. (smokes/ My father/a lot)
7. 그것이 맛이 좋아? (does/ taste/ good/ it/ ?)
8. James는 회사에 운전해서 다닙니다. (drives/ James/ to work)
9. 그것이 듣기에 좋습니까? (it/ sound/ does/ good/ ?)
10. 저 가수는 유명합니까? (famous/ is/ that singer/ ?)

# Writing Pattern Practice _1형식, 2형식

**1.** 「주어+동사」 1형식

해는 동쪽에서 뜬다. _____

Jane은 일한다. _____

엄마가 요리를 하신다. _____

여기 많은 사람들이 많다. _____


**2.** 「주어+be동사+보어」 2형식

나는 키가 크다. _____

Susan은 매우 피곤하다.(very) _____

그들은 간호사들이다. _____


**3.** 「주어+ look, smell, taste, sound, feel, seem 등 + 보어」 2형식

너 오늘 달라 보인다. _____

너 정말 피곤해 보인다.(very) _____

뭔가 냄새가 나쁜데. _____

그 수프 냄새 좋다. _____

그거 맛 좋니? _____

그거 맛 끝내준다.(terrific) _____

그거 좋게 들려. _____

그 털 코트는 촉감이 부드럽다.(The fur coat~) _____

그거 촉감이 좋지 않은데. _____

그들은 친절한 듯 하다. _____


**4.** 「주어+ become, get, turn, grow 등 + 보어」 2형식

나는 의사가 될 거야.(become) _____

Susan은 가수가 되었다.(become) _____

나는 배고파졌다.(get) _____

Laura는 지루해졌다.(get) _____

잎들이 빨갛게 물들었다.(turn) _____

어두워졌다.(grow) _____

# 11 | 3형식

A: What will you do this weekend?
B: I'll watch a ball game on TV. How about you?
A: I think I will go to a movie.
B: That sounds good.

*ball game 야구경기

**1.** 3형식문장은 「주어+동사+목적어」의 형태로 동작의 대상이 되는 목적어가 항상 뒤따르게 된다.

I have **a car**. 나는 자동차를 가지고 있다.
I know **how to use it**. 나는 그것을 어떻게 사용하는지 안다.
Jane said **that she was OK**. Jane은 괜찮다고 말했다.

**2.** 3형식의 목적어 역할을 하는 명사는 다음과 같다.

● 일반명사
I love **apples**. 나는 사과를 좋아한다.
Most people eat **too much meat**. 대부분의 사람들은 너무 많은 고기를 먹는다.

● 대명사
"Do you like apples?" "Yes, I like **them** very much." 너는 사과를 좋아하니?
응, 나는 사과를 매우 좋아해.

● 동명사
Neil enjoys **swimming**. Neil은 수영하는 것을 즐긴다.
Would you mind **opening** the window? 창문 열어주시겠어요?

● to부정사
I want **to go** on a diet. 나는 다이어트 하는 것을 원한다.
I decided **to move** to New York. 나는 뉴욕으로 이사 가는 것을 결심했다.

● 기타 명사구
Do you know **where to go**? 너는 어디를 가야할 지 아니?
I learned **how to use this machine**. 나는 어떻게 이 기계를 사용하는지 배웠다.

● 명사절
I hope **that you have a great time**. 나는 당신이 좋은 시간 보냈으면 좋겠어요.
I want to know **if he likes me**. 나는 그가 나를 좋아하는지 알고 싶다.
I want to know **what her phone number is**. 나는 그녀의 전화번호가 무엇인지 알고 싶다.

# Unit Test

**1.** 다음 문장의 형식을 쓰시오.

| 「주어+동사」 → 1형식 | 「주어+동사+보어」 → 2형식 | 「주어+동사+목적어」 → 3형식 |
|---|---|---|

1. Do you play cards? (      )
2. It snows a lot in the winter. (      )
3. I've studied hard. (      )
4. Do your parents speak English? (      )
5. The weather is nice and warm. (      )
6. We often sleep late on weekends. (      )
7. I don't like big cities. (      )
8. Jane never eats breakfast. (      )
9. There was some misunderstanding. (      )
10. You're wearing a new skirt. (      )

**2.** 다음 문장에서 목적어 역할을 하는 명사/ 명사구/ 명사절에 동그라미 하시오.

1. Jane is wearing a coat.
2. I speak three languages.
3. I don't know how to say this.
4. Do you eat dinner in restaurants a lot?
5. I want to travel by train.
6. Does Sue think that I'm stupid?
7. They know that money is not everything.

**3.** 우리말과 일치하도록 괄호 안의 단어를 알맞게 배열하시오.

1. 그는 수영하는 것을 즐긴다. (swimming/ he/ enjoys )

_____

2. 대부분의 사람들은 너무 많은 패스트푸드를 먹는다. (eat/ most people/fast food/ too much)

_____

3. 너는 스파게티를 어떻게 만드는지 아니? (spaghetti/ you/ know/ do/ how to make/ ?)

_____

4. 나는 네 이름이 무엇인지 안다. (know/ I/ what/ is/ your name)

_____

5. 너는 돈이 중요하다고 생각하니? (money/ do/ think/ you/ important/ that/ is/ ?)

_____

# Writing Pattern Practice _3형식

**1.** 「주어 + 동사 + 목적어(일반명사)」

나는 자동차를 가지고 있다.

나는 사과를 좋아한다.

너 모자를 쓰고 있구나.(wear)

Janet은 3개 국어를 한다.

대부분의 사람들은 너무 많은 고기를 먹는다.(too much)


**2.** 「주어 + 동사 + 목적어(대명사)」

Do you like apples? 응, 나는 그것들을 매우 좋아해.

Did you bring your umbrella? 아니, 그것을 안 가져왔는데.


**3.** 「주어 + 동사 + 목적어(동명사)」

나는 일하는 것을 마쳤다.(finish)

Neil은 수영하는 것을 즐긴다.

창문 열어주시겠어요?(Would you mind~)


**4.** 「주어 + 동사 + 목적어(to부정사)」

나는 다이어트 하는 것을 원한다.(go on a diet)

나는 뉴욕으로 이사 가는 것을 결심했다.

Henry는 외식하고 싶어한다.(would like to)


**5.** 「주어 + 동사 + 목적어(기타 명사구)」

나는 어떻게 이 기계를 사용하는지 배웠다.

너는 어디를 가야할 지 아니?(where to go)


**6.** 「주어 + 동사 + 목적어(명사절)」

나는 당신이 좋은 시간 보냈으면 좋겠어요. (hope)

나는 그가 나를 좋아하는지 알고 싶다.(want)

나는 그녀의 전화번호가 무엇인지 알고 싶다.(want)

내 생각에 이번 주말에 영화를 볼 것 같아.

# 12 | 4형식

Grammar
in
Practice

A: Get me something to drink, please.
B: OK. I'll get you some orange juice.
A: I feel like drinking some coffee. Can you make some for me?
B: Sure.

Grammar
in
Use

1. 4형식문장은 목적어가 두개 있다. 「주어+동사+간접목적어+직접목적어」의 형태로 쓰며 '~에게 (간접목적어) …를(직접목적어) 하다' 로 해석한다.
   I'd like to buy <u>you</u> <u>lunch</u>. 나는 너에게 점심을 사주고 싶어.
   간접목적어 직접목적어

2. 4형식에 쓰이는 동사 '~에게 …를 주다' 라는 의미로 쓰이는 teach(가르쳐주다), send(보내주다), tell(말해주다), lend(빌려주다), show(보여주다), buy(사주다), make(만들어주다), write(써주다) 등이다.
   I **gave** him a book. 나는 그에게 책을 주었다.
   My friend **sent** me a postcard. 친구가 나에게 우편엽서를 보냈다.
   Would you **lend** me a pen? 저에게 펜을 하나 빌려주시겠습니까?
   Grandma **told** me a story. 할머니는 나에게 이야기를 들려 주셨다.
   A man **showed** me the way to the bank. 어떤 남자가 나에게 은행까지 길을 알려줬다.
   She **made** her daughter a new dress. 그녀는 딸에게 새 드레스를 만들어 주셨다.
   **Buy** me dinner. 저녁 사.
   Mrs. White **teaches** us English. 화이트 부인이 우리에게 영어를 가르친다.
   Sue **writes** him a letter every week. Sue는 그에게 매주 편지를 쓴다.
   Please **get** me some water. 물을 좀 가져다주세요.

3. 4형식 문장을 3형식으로 바꾸어 쓸 수 있다.
   ● 「주어+동사+간접목적어+직접목적어」 → 「주어+동사+직접목적어+to/for+간접목적어」
   ● to를 사용하는 동사: tell, teach, send, lend, show, write, give
     I gave him a book. 나는 그에게 책을 줬다.
     → I gave a book **to** him.
   ● for를 사용하는 동사: get, buy, make
     My boyfriend bought me a ring. 남자친구가 나에게 반지를 사줬다.
     → My boyfriend bought a ring **for** me.

# Unit Test

**1.** 다음 문장의 형식을 쓰시오.

> 「주어+동사」 → 1형식    「주어+동사+보어」 → 2형식    「주어+동사+목적어」 → 3형식
>
> 「주어+동사+간접목적어+직접목적어」 → 4형식

1. I'll buy you dinner. (      )
2. I gave the keys to Henry. (      )
3. Sue lent her car to me. (      )
4. Does he smoke? (      )
5. Do I look fat? (      )
6. I sent you a postcard. (      )
7. Can you pass me the salt? (      )
8. I hope that you have a good time in Hawaii. (      )
9. Tim brought his mother some flowers. (      )
10. Make us some cake. (      )

**2.** 보기와 같이 4형식 문장 「주어+동사+간접목적어+직접목적어」를 3형식 문장 「주어+동사+직접목적어+to/for+간접목적어」로 바꾸시오.

> 보기 | I gave him some money. → I gave some money to him.

1. Can you lend me some money?
2. Pass me the salt, please.
3. Tell me a funny story.
4. I bought you this watch.
5. Can you give her the books?
6. My girlfriend wrote me a letter.
7. John made me some coffee.

**3.** 우리말과 일치하도록 괄호 안의 단어를 알맞게 배열하시오.

1. 내게 20달러 빌려줄래요? (lend/ 20 dollars/ me/ can you/ ?)

2. 내가 너에게 선물 사 줄게. (I'll/ a present/ buy/ you)

3. 나는 경찰관에게 내 면허증을 보여주었다. (I/ the police officer/ showed/ my driver's license)

# Writing Pattern Practice _4형식

**1.** 「주어 + teach, send, tell, lend, show, buy, make, write, get + 간접목적어 + 직접목적어」

나는 그에게 책을 주었다. _____

친구가 나에게 엽서를 보냈다. _____

학생들은 나에게 몇 가지 질문을 했다. _____

저에게 펜을 하나 빌려주시겠습니까?(Would you~) _____

할머니는 나에게 이야기를 들려 주셨다. _____

어떤 남자가 나에게 은행까지 길을 알려줬다. _____

그녀는 딸에게 새 드레스를 만들어 주었다. _____

나에게 저녁 사. _____

화이트 부인이 우리에게 영어를 가르친다. _____

Sue는 그에게 매주 편지를 쓴다. _____

제게 물을 좀 가져다주세요.(Please~) _____

나는 그녀에게 다음에 무엇을 할지 물어보았다. _____

**2.** 「주어 + tell, teach, send, lend, show, write, give) + 직접목적어 + to + 간접목적어」

그녀는 우리에게 재미있는 얘기를 해 줬다.(funny) _____

내게 돈 좀 빌려줘. _____

그는 나에게 영어를 가르쳐줬다. _____

나는 그에게 책을 줬다. _____

그것을 나에게 보내. _____

**3.** 「주어 + get, buy, make + 직접목적어 + for + 간접목적어」

남자친구가 나에게 반지를 사줬다. _____

그녀는 나에게 물을 좀 갖다 줬다. _____

나는 삼촌에게 커피를 타 드렸다. _____

# 13 | 5형식

A: You look great today.
B: I had my hair permed.
A: It makes you look prettier.
B: Really? Thanks.

1. 5형식문장은 「주어+동사+목적어+목적보어」의 형태로 목적어를 보충 설명하는 목적격보어가 필요하다. 이 때 명사와 형용사 등이 목적격 보어 역할을 한다.

I **found** <u>English</u> <u>fun</u>.
         목적어   목적격보어

People **call** <u>him</u> <u>a fool</u>.
         목적어   목적격보어

2. 5형식에 주로 쓰는 동사는 다음과 같다.

● **지각동사** (see …하는 것을 보다, watch …하는 것을 지켜보다, feel …하는 것을 느끼다, hear …하는 것을 듣다 등)

I **saw** <u>you</u> <u>doze/dozing</u> during the class. 너 수업시간 내내 조는/졸고 있는 거 봤어.
I like to **watch** <u>you</u> <u>dance/dancing</u>. 나는 너 춤추는/춤추고 있는 거 지켜보는 게 좋아.
I **felt** <u>Sally</u> <u>breathe/breathing</u> gently. 나는 Sally가 조용히 숨쉬는/숨쉬고 있는 것을 느꼈다.
I **heard** <u>them</u> <u>fight/fighting</u>. 나는 그들이 싸우는/싸우고 있는 것을 들었다.

● **사역동사** (make …하게 만들다, have …하게 시키다, let …하게 허락하다 등)

You always **make** <u>me</u> <u>smile</u>. 너는 항상 나를 미소 짓게 해.
I **had** <u>my son</u> <u>do</u> the laundry. 나는 아들에게 빨래를 시켰다.
I'm supposed to get home by 9 o'clock. Please **let** <u>me</u> <u>go</u>.
나는 9시까지 집에 가기로 되어있어. 나를 가게 해 줘.

● **기타동사** (call …라고 부르다, name …라고 이름 짓다, find …라는 것을 알다, keep 계속…하게 하다, want …하기를 원하다 등)

**Call** <u>me</u> <u>Katie</u>. 나를 Katie라고 불러줘.
I **named** <u>the dog</u> <u>Mary</u>. 나는 그 개를 Mary라고 이름 지어 줬다.
I **found** <u>Mike</u> <u>nice</u>. 나는 Mike가 괜찮다는 것을 알았다.
I'm sorry to **keep** <u>you</u> <u>waiting</u>. 당신을 계속 기다리게 해서 죄송해요.
Do you **want** <u>me</u> <u>to vacuum</u> the floor? 내가 바닥 진공청소기로 청소해 줄까?

# Unit Test

**1.** 다음 문장의 형식을 쓰시오.

| 「주어+동사」 → 1형식 | 「주어+동사+보어」 → 2형식 | 「주어+동사+목적어」 → 3형식 |
|---|---|---|
| 「주어+동사+간접목적어+직접목적어」 → 4형식 | | 「주어+동사+목적어+목적보어」 → 5형식 |

1. My mother bought me many kinds of novels. (          )
2. I found the store to be cheap and good. (          )
3. Coffee keeps me awake. (          )
4. I heard her cry. (          )
5. Do you get up early? (          )
6. Something smells bad. (          )
7. You always make me happy. (          )
8. I opened a window. (          )
9. The movie made me sad. (          )
10. I'll get you something to eat. (          )

**2.** 둘 중 알맞은 것에 동그라미 하시오.

1. I saw them (dance/ to dance)
2. Jimmy always makes me (smile/ smiling)
3. My mother had me (wash/ to wash) the dishes.
4. Let her (go/ going)
5. I heard them (fight/ to fight)

**3.** 우리말과 일치하도록 괄호 안의 단어를 알맞게 배열하시오.

1. Richard는 나를 항상 행복하게 만든다.(always/ happy/ makes/ Richard/ me)

_____

2. 너는 내가 춤추는 거 봤어? (did/ me/ see/ you/dance/ ?)

_____

3. 엄마가 나에게 방청소를 시키셨어. (my mother/ me/ had/ clean up the room)

_____

4. 나는 그 아기가 자고 있는 것을 지켜보았어. (the baby/ I/ watched/ sleeping)

_____

5. 사람들은 그를 Mr. Perfect이라고 부른다. (him/ people/ call/ Mr. Perfect)

_____

6. 나는 그가 거짓말쟁이라는 것을 알았다. (found/ I/ him/ a liar/ to be)

_____

7. 제가 제 소개할게요. (let/ myself/ introduce/ me)

_____

# Writing Pattern Practice _5형식

**1.** 「주어 + see/ watch/ feel/ hear + 목적어 + 동사원형/ 동사+ing」

나는 네가 조는 거 봤어.(doze) _____

너희들이 Lisa가 커닝하는 거 봤니? _____

나는 네가 춤추고 있는 거 지켜보는 게 좋아. _____

사람들은 내가 노래 부르는 것을 지켜봤다. _____

나는 Sally가 우는 것을 느꼈다. _____

나는 뭔가 움직이는 것을 느꼈다. _____

나는 그들이 싸우는 것을 들었다.(fight) _____

너는 그가 나가는 소리를 들었니? _____

**2.** 「주어 + make/ have/ let + 목적어 + 동사원형」

너는 항상 나를 미소 짓게 만들어. _____

내가 너를 피곤하게 만들었니? _____

나는 아들에게 빨래하라고 시켰다.(do the laundry) _____

나를 가게 해줘요.(Please~) _____

제가 제 소개할게요. _____

**3.** 「주어 + call/ name + 목적어 + 명사」

나를 Katie라고 불러줘. _____

사람들은 그를 바보라고 부른다.(a fool) _____

나는 그 개를 Mary라고 이름 지어 줬다. _____

누가 너에게 Christine이라고 이름 지어 줬니? _____

**4.** 「주어 + find + 목적어 + 형용사/ 명사」

나는 Mike가 좋은 사람이라는 것을 알았다.(nice) _____

너는 Cindy가 거짓말쟁이라는 것을 알았니? _____

**5.** 「주어 + keep + 목적어 + 형용사」

커피는 나를 계속 깨어있게 해요.(awake) _____

당신을 계속 기다리게 해서 죄송해요. _____

**6.** 「주어 + want + 목적어 + to부정사」

바닥 진공청소기로 청소해 줄까요?(vacuum) _____

나는 네가 가수가 되었으면 좋겠어. _____

# REVIEW 1

**1.** 다음 문장의 형식을 쓰시오.

| 「주어+동사」→1형식 | 「주어+동사+보어」→2형식 | 「주어+동사+목적어」→3형식 |
|---|---|---|
| 「주어+동사+간접목적어+직접목적어」→4형식 | | 「주어+동사+목적어+목적보어」→5형식 |

① I exercise at a gym. (　　　　)

② You sometimes make me embarrassed. (　　　　)

③ Give me a hand. (　　　　)

④ I want to eat out. (　　　　)

⑤ You look pretty. (　　　　)

⑥ Give it to me. (　　　　)

⑦ Did I make you feel tired? (　　　　)

⑧ Do I look different today? (　　　　)

⑨ I want to know if he likes me. (　　　　)

⑩ You're wearing a new skirt. (　　　　)

⑪ Please get me some water. (　　　　)

⑫ I found Mike nice. (　　　　)

⑬ There are a lot of people here. (　　　　)

⑭ Something smells good. (　　　　)

⑮ Coffee keeps me awake. (　　　　)


**2.** 둘 중에서 알맞은 것을 골라 동그라미 하시오.

① You look (tired/ tire).

② It sounds (interest/ interesting).

③ Lisa got (happy/ happily)

④ The fur coat feels (soft/ softly).

⑤ I love (eat/ eating) apples.

⑥ Do you enjoy (play/ playing) tennis?

⑦ I gave a book (to/ at) Michael.

⑧ He wrote a letter (to/ at) me.

⑨ My father bought a watch (to/ for) me.

⑩ Can you make some coffee (to/ for) me?


**3.** 다음 문장에서 목적어 역할을 하는 것에 동그라미 하시오.

① I met one of my friends on my way here.

② I want to know if he will leave for Florida.

③ You always make me smile.

④ Do you want to leave?

⑤ I found Susie to be honest.

**1.** 「주어+동사(+부사(구))」로 이루어진 문장을 고르시오.

① I eat breakfast at 8.
② I saw you dance.
③ Do you want to stay here?
④ Karl gets up at 7.
⑤ Don't make me tired.

**2.** 「주어+동사+보어」로 이루어진 문장을 고르시오.

① Something smells really bad.
② He kept me waiting.
③ Did I bother you?
④ I go to bed late.
⑤ Get me some food.

**3.** 「주어+동사+목적어」로 이루어진 문장을 고르시오.

① You look tired.
② There is something to eat here.
③ I think he is single.
④ Bring me some flowers.
⑤ Please call me Ted.

**4.** 「주어+동사+간접목적어+직접목적어」로 이루어진 문장을 고르시오.

① Sally wrote me a letter.
② Give it to me.
③ Do I look bored?
④ I eat a lot.
⑤ Tim makes me happy all the time.

**5.** 「주어+동사+목적어+보어」로 이루어진 문장을 고르시오.

① It's warm today.
② That fur coat looks expensive.
③ I want to eat noodles.
④ My mother doesn't let me go out much.
⑤ Give me a call.

[6~7] 빈칸에 들어갈 알맞은 말을 고르시오.

**6.** Susan told _____ a funny story.

① we      ② our
③ us      ④ ours
⑤ it

**7.** Do you want me _____ ?

① vacuum the floor
② to vacuum the floor
③ that vacuum the floor
④ if vacuum the floor
⑤ whether vacuum the floor

**8.** 다음 글을 읽고 밑줄 친 문장 중 「주어+동사+목적어+보어」로 이루어진 5형식 문장을 고르시오.

 ①Many people show their love by giving chocolate. ②They think chocolate is some kind of a symbol of love.

You know what? Chocolate truly could be related to love! Researchers have found that eating chocolate makes something happen in our brains. ③It makes us feel happy and excited. Chocolate produces the same feelings that we have when we love someone.

So, ④do you feel lonely? ⑤Are you without a boyfriend or girlfriend? Just eat some chocolate!

*researcher 연구원 *produce 생산하다

# *Chapter 4 | 동사

Be동사 | Unit 14

일반동사 | Unit 15

조동사 can/ could | Unit 16

조동사 may/ might | Unit 17

조동사 will/ would | Unit 18

조동사 shall/ should/ had better | Unit 19

조동사 must/ have to/ have got to | Unit 20

# 14 | Be 동사

Grammar
in
Practice

A: What's your name?
B: My name is Jack.
A: Are you from the United States?
B: No, I am not. I'm from Canada.
A: Are you married?
B: Yes, I am. My wife is an English teacher.

---

Grammar
in
Use

● Be동사의 축약형

| | 긍정 | | 부정 | |
|---|---|---|---|---|
| 단수 | I am<br>you are<br>he is<br>she is<br>it is | I'm<br>you're<br>he's<br>she's<br>it's | I am not<br>you are not<br>he is not<br>she is not<br>it is not | I'm not<br>you're not 또는 you aren't<br>he's not 또는 he isn't<br>she's not 또는 she isn't<br>it's not 또는 it isn't |
| 복수 | we are<br>you are<br>they are | we're<br>you're<br>they're | we are not<br>you are not<br>they are not | we're not 또는 we aren't<br>you're not 또는 you aren't<br>they're not 또는 they aren't |

**1.** be동사는 '~이다'의 뜻으로 주어의 인칭과 수에 따라 am, are, is를 쓴다.
I'**m** a student. 나는 학생이다.
It'**s** eight thirty. You'**re** late again. 8시 반이야. 너 또 늦었다.
He'**s** inside. 그는 안에 있다.

**2.** be동사의 부정은 뒤에 not을 붙인다.
I'**m not** hungry. 나는 배고프지 않다.
She'**s not** sad. 그녀는 슬프지 않다.

**3.** be동사 다음에는 주로 명사나 형용사(분사) 또는 장소를 나타내는 부사 등이 온다.
My father is **a professor**.(명사) 우리 아버지는 교수다.
I'm **happy**.(형용사) 나는 행복하다.
She's **tired**.(분사) 그녀는 피곤하다.
John is **downstairs**.(장소부사) John은 아래층에 있다.

**| MORE TIPS |** 장소를 나타내는 부사는 here(여기에), there(저기에), home(집에), upstairs(위층에),
downstairs(아래층에), inside(안에), outside(밖에) 등이 있다.

## Unit Test

**1.** 빈칸에 알맞은 be동사(am, are, is)를 넣으시오.

1. I _____ a teacher. I teach English.
2. The weather _____ nice today.
3. John _____ afraid of dogs.
4. These flowers _____ beautiful.
5. Tom and I _____ close friends.

**2.** Page 50의 Dialogue를 보고 남자(B)에 관하여 알맞은 답을 하시오.

1. What's his name?(이름) His name _____ _____ .
2. Is he from the United States?(출신) No, he _____ _____ .
3. Where is he from?(출신) He _____ _____ _____.
4. Is he married?(결혼) Yes, he _____ .
5. What's her job?(부인의 직업) She _____ _____ _____ _____ .

**3.** 그림을 보고 보기에서 알맞은 단어를 골라 적절하게 문장을 완성하시오.

보기 | hungry    upstairs    married

1. He _____ .    2. They _____ .    3. She _____ .

**4.** 보기의 단어와 be동사 (am/ am not/ is/ isn't/ are/ aren't)를 사용하여 문장을 완성하시오.

보기 | ugly   diligent(부지런한)   nice   fun   six   upstairs   Australian   poor   closed   heavy

1. Let's go out. The weather _____ .
2. I don't like computer games. They _____ .
3. She always gets up late. She _____ .
4. Those people aren't American. They _____ .
5. Mr. Wilson is rich. He _____ .
6. "Is your sister pretty?" "No, she _____ ."
7. "What time is it?" "It _____ ."
8. "May I help you?" "Yes, please. These bags _____ ."
9. "Where is Nancy?" "She _____ ."
10. "Is the store open?" "No, it _____ ."

# Writing Pattern Practice

**1.** 「I'm + 형용사」 '나는 …이다.'

나는 오늘 피곤해. _____

너는 예쁘구나. _____

너희들은 매우 부지런하구나. _____

Sally는 개를 두려워한다.(be afraid of) _____

8시 반이야. 너 또 늦었다. _____


**2.** 「I'm not + 형용사」 '나는 …이 아니다.'

나는 배고프지 않다. _____

그녀는 슬프지 않다. _____

오늘은 날씨가 좋지 않다.(nice) _____

우리는 건강하지 않다.(healthy) _____


**3.** 「I'm + 명사」 '나는 …다.'

나는 학생이다. _____

너는 바보다.(a fool) _____

그들은 변호사들이다. _____

Tom과 나는 친한 친구다.(close) _____


**4.** 「I'm not + 명사」 '나는 …가 아니다.'

나는 뚱뚱하지 않다. _____

너는 천재가 아니다.(a genius) _____

그는 경찰관이 아니다.(a police officer) _____

그 사람들은 미국사람이 아니야.(Those~) _____


**5.** 「I'm + 장소부사」 '나는 …에 있다.'

나는 위층에 있다. _____

너 집에 있구나. _____

그는 안에 있다. _____

Tom과 Jerry는 밖에 있어. _____

여기에는 아무도 없다.(Nobody~) _____


**6.** 「I'm not + 장소부사」 '나는 …에 있지 않다.'

나는 집에 있지 않다. _____

John은 아래층에 있지 않다. _____

Ted는 여기 있지 않다. _____

그들은 밖에 있지 않다.(outside) _____

# 15 일반동사

A: Would you like some coffee?

B: No, thanks. I don't drink coffee. I'd like some tea.

> Q: Does she like coffee?
> A: No, she doesn't drink coffee.
> Q: What does she want to drink?
> A: She wants to drink some tea.

**1.** 일반동사는 주어의 인칭, 수 그리고 문장의 시제에 따라 형태가 변한다.

<u>Everybody</u> **likes** music. (3인칭 단수 주어일 때 동사원형에 –(e)s를 붙인다.) 모두 음악을 좋아한다.
every– :단수취급

I **had** dinner with my family. (동사과거형은 동사원형에 –(e)d를 붙이거나 불규칙하게 변한다.)
나는 가족과 함께 저녁을 먹었다.

**2.** 일반동사의 부정은 주어가 I/you/we/they일 경우 동사원형 앞에 do not(don't)을 he/she/it일 경우 does not(doesn't)을 쓴다.

We **don't** watch television very often. 우리는 텔레비전을 그렇게 자주 보지는 않는다.

Sarah drinks Sprite, but she **doesn't** drink Coke. Sarah는 사이다는 마시지만 콜라는 마시지 않는다.

**3.** 주어의 행동을 나타내는 동작 동사가 있다. : go, come, eat, drink, walk, run, write 등

I always **eat** breakfast. 나는 항상 아침을 먹는다.

Cindy **walks** her dog every day. Cindy는 매일 개를 산책시킨다.

My father **drinks** too much coffee. 아버지는 커피를 너무 많이 드신다.

**4.** 주어의 상태를 나타내는 상태동사가 있다. 일반적으로 진행형을 쓰지 않는다. : like, prefer(더 좋아하다), need, want, hate, know, seem, believe, fit(치수 등이 맞다), understand, belong(~에 속하다) 등

I **know** his phone number. 나는 그의 전화번호를 알고 있다.

Mary **likes** movies. Mary는 영화를 좋아한다.

**5.** 동사의 형태가 변형되어 명사, 형용사, 부사의 역할을 하기도 한다.

- 명사역할 　I like **to play** soccer. (play) 나는 축구하는 것을 좋아한다.
　　　　　**Playing** soccer is fun. (play) 축구하는 것은 재미있다.

- 형용사역할 　I'm **bored**. (bore) 나는 지루하다.
　　　　　This movie is so **boring**. (bore) 이 영화는 지겹다.

- 부사역할 　I came here **to see** Mr. Smith. (see) 저는 Smith씨를 만나러 왔는데요.
　　　　　It's nice **to see** you here. (see) 여기서 당신을 봐서 반가워요.

# Unit Test

**1.** 알맞은 동사 형태에 동그라미 하시오.

1. David (listen/ listens) to classical music.

2. Everybody (like/ likes) soccer in Korea.

3. I (love/ loves) big cities.

4. It (rain/ rains) a lot in the summer.

5. Henry and I (do/ does) a lot of different things in our free time.

**2.** 틀린 곳을 찾아 고치시오.

1. I'm believing in God.                         →

2. The bag is belonging to my brother.          →

3. Which one are you preferring?                 →

4. Tim is wanting a new car.                     →

5. My mother is understanding me.               →

6. I'm hating to exercise.                       →

7. Is Kate liking to see a movie?                →

8. Ken is knowing French and Spanish.           →

9. You are seeming to be in good health.        →

10. This jacket is fitting.                       →

**3.** 글에서 일반동사를 찾아 밑줄치시오.

Kate is one of my close friends. She works two part-time jobs and likes buying second-hand clothes because they don't cost much. Her dream is becoming a teacher. I hope that she can achieve her goal.

*achieve 성취하다, 달성하다

**4.** 긍정문을 부정문으로 고치시오.

1. I play the violin very well.           →

2. My sister plays the piano very well.   →

3. John hates to cook.                    →

4. You work very hard.                    →

5. My parents enjoy playing golf.         →

70

# Writing Pattern Practice

**1.** 「I/You/We/They + 일반동사」 '나는/너는/우리는/그들은 …한다'

나는 축구를 좋아한다.　　　　　　　　　　　_____

나는 그의 전화번호를 알고 있다.　　　　　_____

너는 여자친구가 있구나.　　　　　　　　　_____

우리는 매일 조깅간다.(go jogging)　　　　_____

그들은 항상 아침을 먹는다.　　　　　　　　_____

**2.** 「She/He/It + 일반동사+(e)s」 '그녀는/그는/그것은 …한다'

모두가 음악을 좋아한다.　　　　　　　　　_____

아무도 상관하지 않는다.(care)　　　　　　_____

Cindy는 개를 매일 산책시켜요.(walk)　　　_____

아버지는 커피를 많이 드신다.(a lot)　　　　_____

James는 영화를 좋아한다.　　　　　　　　　_____

겨울에는 눈이 많이 온다.(a lot)　　　　　　_____

제주도에는 비가 많이 온다.(a lot, on)　　　_____

**3.** 「I/You/We/They + don't +동사원형」 '나는/너는/우리는/그들은 …안한다'

나는 운동을 하지 않는다.　　　　　　　　　　　　_____

너는 채소를 먹지 않는구나.(vegetables)　　　　　_____

우리는 텔레비전을 그렇게 자주 보지는 않는다.(very often)　_____

그들은 많은 돈을 가지고 있지 않다.(much)　　　_____

우리 부모님은 늦잠을 주무시지 않는다.(sleep in)　_____

**4.** 「She/He/It + doesn't + 동사원형」 '그녀는/그는/그것은 …안한다'

Sally는 고기를 먹지 않는다.　　　　　　　　_____

내 남동생은 콜라를 마시지 않는다.　　　　　_____

동경에는 눈이 많이 오지 않는다.(much)　　　_____

그 텔레비전은 작동하지 않는다.(work)　　　_____

# 16 조동사 can/could

A: What can I do for you?
B: Could you change a ten-dollar bill?
A: Of course. Here you are.

**1.** 조동사는 본동사를 도와 보조역할을 한다. 조동사 뒤에는 항상 동사원형을 쓴다. 부정문은 조동사 뒤에 not을 붙이고 의문문은 「조동사+주어+동사원형?」 어순으로 쓴다.

**2.** can은 '~할 수 있다' 라는 능력을 나타낸다.
I **can** ski. 나는 스키 탈줄 안다.
He **can** speak French very well. 그는 불어를 매우 잘한다.
I can't make spaghetti. 나는 스파게티 만들 줄 모른다.
**Can** you play the piano? 피아노 칠 줄 알아?

**3.** can은 '~해도 좋다' 라는 허락을 나타낸다.
You **can** park here. 당신은 여기에 주차해도 좋아요.
You **can't** swim here. 여기서 수영하면 안돼요.
**Can** I ask your name? 이름 물어봐도 될까요?

**4.** can은 부정문이나 의문문에서 '~일리 없다', '과연~일까?' 라는 강한 의심을 나타내기도 한다. cannot 또는 축약형 can't을 쓴다.
It **can't** be possible. 그것이 가능할 리 없어.
**Can** she be married? 그녀가 과연 결혼했을까?

**5.** could는 can의 과거형으로 '~할 수 있었다' 라는 뜻으로 쓴다.
I **couldn't** buy a toy for my daughter because I had no money.
나는 돈이 없어서 딸에게 장난감을 사줄 수 없었다.
I had a birthday party, but Shiela **couldn't** come.
내 생일파티가 있었는데 Shiela는 올 수 없었다.

**6.** could는 '~일 수도 있다' 라는 약한 추측을 나타낸다.
It **could** be Cathy's. 그것은 Cathy의 것일 수도 있다.
Catherine **could** be at work. Catherine이 일하고 있을 수도 있다.

**7.** could는 누군가에게 부탁의 말을 할 때 can보다 공손하게 사용할 수 있다.
**Could** I have your e-mail address? 이메일 주소가 어떻게 되시나요?
**Could** you give me a ride home? 집에까지 태워다 주시겠어요?
**Could** you change a ten-dollar bill? 10달러 지폐 바꿔 줄 수 있어요?

# Unit Test

**1.** 다음은 John이 할 수 있는 일과 없는 일이다. can과 can't을 이용해 문장을 만드시오.

1.
swim

2.
ride a horse

3.
drive

4.
ski

1. He _____

2. He _____

3. He _____

4. He _____

**2.** 보기의 동사에 can 또는 can't 을 붙여 문장을 완성하시오.

보기 | tell   come   taste   help   speak

1. This suitcase is so heavy. _____ you _____ me?

2. There is some cake left. You _____ some.

3. I'm sorry, but I _____ to your party.

4. Olive got the job because she _____ five languages.

5. It's a secret. I _____ you anything now.

**3.** 우리말과 일치하도록 괄호 안의 단어를 알맞게 배열하시오.

1. 내가 여기 앉아도 될까요? (I/ can/ sit/ here/ ?)

2. 당신은 여기 주차하셔도 좋습니다. (park/ you/ can/ here)

3. 그것이 사실일 리가 없어요. (can't/ it/ true/ be)

4. 제가 커피한잔 마셔도 될까요? (I/ could/ a cup of coffee/ have/ ?)

5. 제가 당신 이름을 알 수 있을까요? (I/ could/ your name/ have/ ?)

6. 나는 한마디도 할 수 없었어요. (couldn't/ a word/ say/ I)

7. 엄마는 영어를 할 줄 모르세요. (can't/ my mother/ speak/ English)

# Writing Pattern Practice

**1.** 「I can/can't + 동사원형」 '나는 …할 수 있다/없다' → 능력

나는 스키 탈줄 안다.

그는 프랑스어를 매우 잘 한다.(French)

나는 스파게티 만들 줄 모른다.(spaghetti)

**2.** 「Can I + 동사원형?」 '내가 …해도 될까?' → 허락

내가 여기에 주차해도 될까?

내가 당신 이름 물어봐도 될까요?

내가 그 전화 사용해도 될까?

너는 여기에 앉아도 돼.

너는 풀장에서 수영해도 돼.(in the pool)

**3.** 「It can't + 동사원형」 '그것은 …일리 없다' → 의심

그것은 사실일 리 없어.

그것이 가능할 리 없어.

그가 결혼했을 리 없어.

**4.** 「I could/couldn't + 동사원형」 '나는 …할 수 있었다/없었다' → 능력(과거)

나는 한마디도 할 수 없었어.(say a word)

Ted는 회의에 참석할 수 없었어.(attend)

우리는 잠을 잘 잘 수 없었어.

**5.** 「I could/couldn't + 동사원형」 '나는 …할(일) 수도 있다/없다' → 추측

나는 그 파티에 갈 수도 있을 거야.

그는 집에 있을 수도 있어.

그것은 Cathy의 가방일 수도 있어.

**6.** 「Could you + 동사원형?」 '…해 주실래요?' → 부탁

저 도와 주실래요?

집에까지 태워다 주시겠어요?(give a ride)

10달러 지폐 바꿔 줄 수 있어요?

# 17 | 조동사 may/might

Grammar in Practice

A: May I ask you a question?

B: Sure.

A: I'm supposed to meet Dr. White here.
   Where can I find him?

B: He might be in the meeting room now.

*be supposed to …하기로 되어 있다

Grammar in Use

**1.** may는 '~해도 좋다' 라는 허락을 나타낸다.

You **may** use my pen. 내 펜을 사용해도 돼.

You **may** not go in. They're having an important meeting.
들어가면 안돼요. 중요한 회의를 하고 있어요.

**May** I take your order? 제가 주문을 받아도 될까요?

**2.** may는 '~일지도 모른다' 는 추측의 의미로 쓴다.

You **may** be tired. 너는 아마 피곤할 거다.

Your coat **may** not be in the closet. It **may** be on the bed.
네 코트가 아마 옷장 안에 없을 거다. 아마 침대 위에 있을 거야.

Take an umbrella. It **may** rain. 우산 가져가. 비가 올지도 몰라.

**3.** might은 may와 비슷한 뜻으로 쓰거나 시제를 일치시킬 때 쓴다.

I **might** go to New York. (추측) 나는 아마 뉴욕으로 갈 거야.

Tom said that his brother **might** be at school.(시제일치)
Tom은 그의 동생이 아마 학교에 있을 거라고 말했다.

# Unit Test

**1.** 대화의 빈칸에 알맞은 말을 쓰시오.

1. A: _____ I use your phone?

   B: Yes, you may.

2. A: May I come in?

   B: Yes, you _____

3. A: May I turn on the TV?

   B: No, you _____ _____


**2.** 다음 문장을 might이 들어간 문장으로 바꿔 쓰시오.

1. Probably I'll see a movie.

   → _____

2. Probably Leo will be here soon.

   → _____

3. Probably Mark is at home.

   → _____

4. Probably it will snow this afternoon.

   → _____

5. Probably there is some misunderstanding.

   → _____


**3.** 다음 문장을 might not이 들어간 문장으로 바꿔 쓰시오.

1. Probably I won't be home until tomorrow.

   → _____

2. Probably it won't rain tomorrow.

   → _____

3. Probably there isn't anybody in there.

   → _____

4. Probably Susan will not come back to Korea.

   → _____

5. Probably it won't be cold tonight.

   → _____


**4.** 보기와 같이 각자 이번 주말 할지도 모를 일을 might을 이용해 적으시오.

| 보기 | I might see a movie with my friends this weekend. |
|---|---|

_____

# Writing Pattern Practice

**1.** 「May I + 동사원형~?」 '내가 …해도 될까요?' → 허락

제가 주문을 받아도 될까요?(take your order) _____

제가 질문 하나 해도 될까요?(ask) _____

제가 메시지 남겨도 될까요?(leave) _____

제가 여기에 앉아도 될까요? _____

제가 당신 이름을 알 수 있을까요?(have) _____

당신은 제 펜을 사용하세요. _____

당신은 여기에 주차해도 좋아요. _____

당신은 내 전화를 써도 좋아요. _____

당신은 여기에서 담배피시면 안돼요. _____


**2.** 「I may + 동사원형~」 '내가 …일지도/할지도 모른다' → 추측

나는 아마 일본에 갈 거야. _____

나는 아마 결석할 거야.(absent) _____

너는 아마 피곤할 거야. _____

네 코트가 아마 옷장 안에 있을 거야.(in the closet) _____

Jack이 아마 여기에 올 거야. _____

그들은 아마 여기에 일주일동안 머무를 거야. _____


**3.** 「I might + 동사원형~」 '내가 …일지도/할지도 모른다' → 추측

나는 아마 유럽에 갈 거야.(Europe) _____

나는 아마 늦을 거야. _____

너는 아마 지루할 거야.(bored) _____

네 안경은 아마 책상 위에 있을 거야. _____

Jenny는 아마 자기 방에 있을 거야. _____

내일 아마 눈 올 거야. _____

그것은 아마 사실일 거야. _____

그들은 아마 내일 여기에 도착할 거야.(get) _____

냉장고에 우유가 좀 있을 거야.(in the fridge) _____

# 18 | 조동사 will/would

A: This cart is broken. Would you give me a hand?
B: Certainly, ma'am. I'll carry your bags for you.

**1.** will은 미래의미 외에도 주어의 의지, 고집, 권유, 부탁, 추측(예상) 등의 의미로 쓴다.

I **will** eat spaghetti for lunch. (미래) 나는 점심에 스파게티를 먹을 거야.

I **will** go home now. (의지) 나는 지금 집에 갈 거야.

He **won't** listen to me. (고집) 그는 내말을 들으려고 안한다.

**Will** you have some more coffee? (권유) 커피 좀 드실래요?

**Will** you marry me? (부탁) 저랑 결혼해줄래요?

That **will** be the hottest fashion next year. (추측/예상) 그건 아마 내년에 크게 유행할 거야.

**2.** would는 will과 비슷한 뜻으로 쓰거나 시제를 일치시킬 때 또는 과거의 습관을 말할 때 쓴다.

**Would** you have dinner with me? (권유) 저와 저녁 드실래요?

**Would** you spell that? (부탁) 스펠링 좀 말해주실래요?

I told you that I **would** be absent. (시제일치) 제가 결석할거라고 말씀드렸는데요.

When I was young, I **would** study hard. (과거 일시적인 습관) 어릴 적 열심히 공부하곤 했다.

**I MORE TIPS I** 과거 규칙적인 습관이나 지속적인 상태를 나타낼 때는 would 대신에 used to를 쓴다.
• I **used to** exercise everyday. 나는 매일 운동을 하곤 했었다.
• The Han River **used to** be very clean. 한강은 매우 깨끗했었다.

**3.** would를 이용한 표현으로 would like (to) ~ '~ 하고 싶다'와 would rather~ '차라리 ~하다' 등이 있다.

**"Would you like** some tea?" "Yes, please." 차 드실래요? 네.

**"Would you like** to go out to eat?" "No, **I'd like** to eat in." 나가서 먹고 싶어?
아니, 집에서 먹고 싶어.

**I'd rather** stay home because I don't feel like going out.
그냥 집에 있을래요 왜냐하면 나갈 기분이 아니라서요.

**Would** you **rather** take a taxi? 차라리 택시를 탈래?

# Unit Test

**1.** 빈칸에 will이나 won't를 써넣으시오.

1. I'm late. It _____ happen again.
2. Martin is 15 years old. He _____ be 16 years old next year.
3. "How much will that be?" "That _____ be $25.
4. Wait. I _____ be ready in a minute.
5. Sally _____ say hello to me after our fight.

**2.** will의 쓰임이 같은 것끼리 연결하시오.

1. Will you hand it to me?          That will be 10 dollars each.
2. The door won't open.             Will you buy me some flowers?
3. Will you come to the meeting?    I will eat a sandwich for lunch.
4. This hat will be in the closet.  Will you have some cake?
5. Will you drink some wine?        This car won't move.

**3.** 보기와 같이 주어진 문장을 읽고 상황에 알맞은 질문을 만드시오.

> 보기 | You want to go to the movies with your friend.
>       You say: Would you like to go to the movies?

1. You want to go out to eat with your friend.
   → You say: _____
2. You want to eat some cake with your friend.
   → You say: _____
3. You want to eat some ice cream with your friend.
   → You say: _____
4. You want to go out for a walk with your friend.
   → You say: _____
5. You want to play tennis with your friend.
   → You say: _____

**4.** 빈칸에 'd rather 또는 'd rather not 중 알맞은 것을 골라 쓰시오.

1. I don't want to go out in the cold. I _____ stay home
2. I'm sick. I _____ go to school today.
3. Vicky doesn't want to go to college. She _____ get a job.
4. I have a stomachache. I _____ eat anything.
5. Cindy has a cold. She _____ stay in bed.

# Writing Pattern Practice

**1.** 「I will ~」 '나는 …할 거야' → 미래, 의지

나는 점심에 스파게티를 먹을 거야. _____

나는 지금 집에 갈 거야. _____

Sally는 늦지 않을 거야. _____


**2.** 「You won't ~」 '너는 …안하려고 하는구나' → 고집

그는 내말을 들으려고 안 해.(listen to me) _____

창문이 안 열려. _____

반지가 안 빠져.(come off) _____


**3.** 「Will you ~?」 '너 …할래/ …해줄래?' → 권유, 부탁

너 콜라 좀 마실래?(have) _____

내 부탁 좀 들어줄래?(do me a favor) _____


**4.** 「That will be ~」 '그것은 …일거예요' → 추측, 예상

그것이 이번 여름 최고의 흥행영화가 될거야. _____

그것은 20달러일 거야. _____

그것은 위대한 그림이 될거야. _____


**5.** 「I would ~」 '나는 …하곤 했다' → 과거의 습관

나는 어릴 적 공부를 열심히 하곤 했다. _____

그는 자주 수영가곤 했었지.(go swimming) _____


**6.** 「Would you ~?」 '당신 …하실래요/ …해주실래요?' → 권유, 부탁

저와 저녁 드실래요?(have dinner) _____

그것 스펠링 좀 말해주실래요?(spell) _____


**7.** 「I would like (to 동사원형)」 '나는 …하고 싶다'

나는 외식하고 싶어요.(eat out) _____

당신 차 드실래요?(some tea) _____

당신 산책 가실래요?(go for a walk) _____


**8.** 「I would rather + 동사원형」 '나는 차라리 …하고 싶다'

나는 그냥 집에 있을래요.(stay) _____

나는 차라리 거기 안 갈래. _____

너 차라리 taxi를 탈래?(take) _____

# 19 | 조동사 shall/ should/ had better

Grammar
in
Practice

A: Shall we finish this tomorrow?

B: No, we should *get this done today. We'd better hurry up.

A: Let's take a coffee break for a while, shall we?

B: No, we don't have much time. Let's just keep on working.

*get this done 이것을 끝마치다

Grammar
in
Use

**1.** shall은 미래의 의미보다 상대방 의향을 물을 때 주로 쓴다.

**Shall** I sit here? 여기 앉아도 될까요?

**Shall** we dance? 우리 춤출까요?

**Shall** we talk about it later? 우리 그것에 대해서 다음에 얘기할까요?

**2.** shall은 Let's로 시작하는 문장의 부가의문문에 덧붙여 쓴다.

Let's go for a walk, **shall** we? 우리 산책가죠, 그럴까요?

Let's go hiking, **shall** we? 우리 하이킹가요, 그럴까요?

**3.** should는 '~해야 한다'는 충고나 조언의 의미로 쓴다.

You **should** see a doctor. 너는 진찰을 받아야 해.

**Should** I dress up? 제가 정장을 입어야 하나요?

**4.** should는 '~일 것이다'는 근거가 있는 추측의 의미로도 쓴다.

Tim **should** be at his office at this hour. 이 시간에 Tim은 그의 사무실에 있을 거야.

The remote control **should** be next to the television. 리모콘은 텔레비전 옆에 있을 거야.

**5.** had better는 '~하는 편이 낫다'라는 뜻으로 경고의 의미를 담고 있다.

Mr. Ward is a bit strange. You'**d better** stay away from him.

Ward씨는 조금 이상해. 멀리 하도록 해.

You'**d better** not be absent. 너는 결석하지 않는 게 좋아.

---

**Santa Claus is coming to town.** 𝄞 ♪

You'd better watch out.

You'd better not cry.

You'd better not pout.

I'm telling you why.

Santa Claus is coming to town........

*watch out 조심하다    *pout 삐치다

---

# Unit Test

**1.** 빈칸에 should 또는 shouldn't를 넣어 문장을 완성하시오.

1. It's a nice movie. You _____ go and see it.

2. Sue has a cold. She _____ see a doctor.

3. You have a test tomorrow. You _____ watch too much TV.

4. It's very cold outside. You _____ go out.

5. That sweater is too expensive. You _____ buy it.

6. Anne doesn't like her job. She _____ get another.

7. You are overweight. You _____ eat so much.

8. Karen is still sick in bed. She _____ go to school.

9. You and I are too young. We _____ drink alcohol.

10. Thai food is very delicious. You _____ try it.


**2.** 빈칸에 'd better 또는 'd better not을 넣어 문장을 완성하시오.

1. Smoking is not good for your health. You _____ quit.

2. You _____ drink the tea right now. It's too hot.

3. You _____ touch the dog. It could bite you.

4. The baby is sleeping. You _____ be quiet.

5. Be careful! You _____ watch out for cars.  *watch out for cars 차 조심하다


**3.** 우리말과 일치하도록 괄호 안의 단어를 알맞게 배열하시오.

1. 우리 좀 쉴까요? (we/ take/ a break/ shall/ ?)

_____

2. 너는 거짓말을 해선 안 된다. (should/ you/ not/ lie)

_____

3. 그녀는 진찰을 받아야 한다. (should/ a doctor/ see/ she)

_____

4. 너희들은 조용히 하는 게 좋아. (better/ had/ you/ quiet/ be)

_____

5. 너는 울지 않는 게 좋아. (had/ better/ you/ not cry)

_____

82

# Writing Pattern Practice

**1.** 「Shall we ~?」 '우리 …할까요?'

제가 여기 앉아도 될까요? _____

제가 창문을 닫아도 될까요? _____

우리 춤출까요? _____

우리 그것에 대해서 다음에 얘기할까요? _____


**2.** 「Let's ~, shall we~?」 '…하자, 그럴까?'

우리 산책 나가죠, 그럴까요?(go for a walk) _____

우리 저녁 먹죠, 그럴까요? _____

우리 쉬죠, 그럴까요?(take a break) _____

우리 지금 떠나죠, 그럴까요? _____


**3.** 「You should ~」 '너는 …해야 한다'

너는 진찰을 받아야 해.(see a doctor) _____

너는 거기에 정각에 가야해.(be, on time) _____

너는 TV를 너무 많이 보지 않아야 해. _____

제가 정장을 입어야 하나요?(dress up) _____


**4.** 「You should」 '너는 …일 거야'

너는 피곤할 거야. _____

이 시간에 Tim은 그의 사무실에 있을 거야.(at this hour) _____

리모콘은 텔레비전 옆에 있을 거야. _____


**5.** 「You'd better (not)~」 '너는 …하는(하지 않는) 편이 낫다'

너 조심하는 게 좋아.(watch out) _____

너 지하철 타는 편이 나아. _____

너 결석하지 않는 게 좋아. _____

너 늦지 않는 게 좋아. _____

너 울지 않는 게 좋아. _____

Unit

# 20 | 조동사 must/ have to/ have got to

Grammar
in
Practice

A: I have to go on a diet. I weigh over 60 kg.

B: No, you don't have to. I think you look just fine.

A: *Do you mean it?

B: Of course.

* Do you mean it? 진심이야?

---

Grammar
in
Use

**1.** must는 '~를 꼭 해야 한다' 라는 뜻으로 강한 의무를 나타낸다. 부정은 must not(mustn't)로 '~를 하면 절대 안 된다' 이다.

You **must** fasten your seatbelt. 안전벨트를 매야 해요.

You **must** not drink and drive. 음주운전을 하면 안돼요.

**Must** we study English? 우리는 영어공부를 해야 하나요?

**2.** must는 '~임에 틀림없다' 라는 강한 추측의 뜻으로도 쓴다. 부정은 cannot be(can't be)로 '~일 리가 없다' 이다.

It **must** be true. 그것은 사실임에 틀림없다.

Jack **must** be in his room. Jack은 자기 방에 있음에 틀림없다.

You **must** weigh over 50kg. 너는 50kg 넘게 나감에 틀림없다.

There **must** be a lot of people on Friday night. 금요일 밤에는 사람이 많이 있음에 틀림없다.

Gary **can't** be married. Gary가 결혼했을 리가 없다.

**3.** have to는 '~ 해야 한다' 라는 뜻으로 의무를 나타낸다. must의 과거형/미래형이 없기 때문에 이를 대신하기도 한다. 부정은 don't have to로 '~할 필요가 없다' 라는 뜻이다.

It's very late. I **have to** go right now. 너무 늦었어. 지금 당장 가야해.

Tom has a test tomorrow. He **has to** study. Tom은 내일 시험이 있다. 그는 공부해야 한다.

Do you really **have to** leave now? 너는 지금 정말 가야하니?

You **don't have to** wait for me. 너는 나를 기다릴 필요가 없어.

Heather **had to** attend the meeting. Heather는 회의에 참석해야 했다.

You **didn't have to** pay for it. 너는 그것을 계산할 필요가 없었어.

Susie **will have to** go and see Mrs. Wilson. Susie는 Wilson 부인을 만나러 가야할 거야.

**4.** have got to는 '~해야 한다' 또는 '~임에 틀림없다' 의 뜻으로 편안한 회화체에서 주로 사용한다.

I'**ve got to** go. 나는 가야해.

**Have** you **got to** go? 너는 가야해?

You've **got to** be joking. 너는 농담하고 있음에 틀림없다.

# Unit Test

**1.** 보기와 같이 표지판을 보고 must 또는 must not을 이용하여 표현하시오.

1. You _____ park here.

2. You _____ enter.

3. You _____ stop.

4. You _____ turn left.

5. You _____ turn right.

6. You _____ fasten your seat belt.


**2.** (　　　)안의 표현을 이용하여 반대 문장을 만들어 보시오.

1. You must stay here. (must not)

2. I don't have to get up early. (have to)

3. Jack must be at work. (cannot)

4. It cannot be true. (must)

5. You must not stay up all night. (must)

*stay up all night 밤새다


**3.** 우리말과 일치하도록 괄호 안의 단어를 알맞게 배열하시오.

1. 너는 여기서 기다려야해. (have got to/ here/ you/ wait)

2. 제가 이것을 내일까지 끝마쳐야하나요? (I/ must/ by tomorrow/ finish/ this/ ?)

3. Kim은 토요일에 일해야 합니까? (have to/ on Saturdays/ does/ Kim/ work/ ?)

# Writing Pattern Practice

**1.** 「You must ~」'너는 …를 꼭 해야 한다'

당신은 안전벨트를 매야 해요.(fasten your seatbelt) _____

우리는 영어공부를 해야 하나요? _____

**2.** 「You must not ~」'너는 …를 하면 (절대) 안 된다'

당신은 음주운전을 하면 안돼요.(drink and drive) _____

당신은 여기에 주차하셔서는 안돼요. _____

**3.** 「You must ~」는 '너는 …임에 틀림없다'

그것은 사실임에 틀림없어. _____

Jack은 자기 방에 있음에 틀림없어. _____

너는 50kg 넘게 나감에 틀림없어.(weigh) _____

금요일 밤에는 여기에 사람이 많이 있음에 틀림없어. _____

**4.** 「You cannot (can't ) ~」'너는 …일 리가 없다'

Gary가 결혼했을 리가 없어. _____

그것이 사실일 리가 없어. _____

**5.** 「You have to ~」'너는 …를 해야 한다'

나는 지금 당장 가야해. _____

Jin은 공부해야해. _____

너는 지금 정말 가야하니? _____

우리는 회의에 참석해야 했어.(과거)(attend) _____

Susie는 Wilson부인을 만나러 가야할 거야.(미래) _____

**6.** 「You don't have to ~」'너는 …할 필요가 없다'

너는 나를 기다릴 필요가 없어. _____

너는 그것을 계산할 필요가 없었어.(pay for) _____

**7.** 「You have got to ~」'…해야 한다'

너는 숙제를 해야 해. _____

나는 가야해. _____

너는 지금 가야해? _____

**8.** 「You've got to ~」' …임에 틀림없다'

너는 농담하고 있음에 틀림없어.(be joking) _____

저 가방은 틀림없이 비싸.(That~) _____

James는 집에 있음에 틀림없어. _____

# WRAP-UP | 조동사

| 의미 | 패턴 | 예문 |
|---|---|---|
| 미래 | I will ~. | I will be there in an hour. |
| 부탁,<br>정중한 부탁 | Can you~?<br>Will you~?<br>Could you~?<br>Would you~?<br>May I ~? | Can you give me a hand?<br>Will you give me a hand?<br>Could you help me?<br>Would you help me?<br>May I sit here? |
| 능력 | I can ~.<br>I can't ~. | I can swim.<br>I can't swim. |
| 추측 | He could~.   ↑ 0%<br>He might~.<br>He may~.<br>He should~.<br>He's got to~.<br>He must ~.   ↓ 100% | He could be tired.<br>He might be tired.<br>He may be tired.<br>He should be tired.<br>He's got to be tired.<br>He must be tired. |
| 의심 | You can't ~. | You can't be a student. |
| 충고 | You should ~. | You should see a doctor. |
| 경고 | You'd better~. | You'd better leave now. |
| 의무 | You must~.<br>You have to~.<br>You have got to ~. | You must fasten your seat belt.<br>You have to do your best.<br>You've got to save some money. |
| 불필요 | You don't have to~. | You don't have to stay with me. |
| 금지 | You must not~. | You must not park here. |

**1.** 틀린 곳을 바르게 고치시오.

① Everybody like music. → _____

② It rain a lot in the summer. → _____

③ I'm knowing his phone number. → _____

④ Are you liking movies? → _____

⑤ We're understanding you. → _____

⑥ Sally don't eat meat. → _____

⑦ My parents doesn't sleep in. → _____

⑧ He can speaks English very well. → _____

⑨ There might is some water on the table. → _____

⑩ I'd like to some coffee. → _____

**2.** 다음 문장을 영어로 쓰시오.

① John은 아래층에 있다. → _____

② 그들은 의사들이다. → _____

③ 나는 차라리 택시 탈래. → _____

④ 창문이 안 열려요. → _____

⑤ 너는 결석하지 않는 게 좋아.(경고) → _____

**3.** 다음 문장을 우리말로 쓰시오.

① You can park here. → _____

② That will be $20. → _____

③ It can't be possible. → _____

④ You must weigh over 50 kg. → _____

⑤ You've got to be joking. → _____

**4.** 문장을 괄호안의 지시대로 바꾸시오.

① John is upstairs. (부정문으로) → _____

② We watch television often. (부정문으로) → _____

③ You'd better go there. (부정문으로) → _____

④ I can make spaghetti.(부정문으로) → _____

⑤ We're not tired. (긍정문으로) → _____

⑥ You must not turn left here. (긍정문으로) → _____

⑦ It couldn't be true. (긍정문으로) → _____

⑧ I'd rather not stay here.(긍정문으로) → _____

**1.** 어법상 맞는 문장을 고르시오.

① She and I am friends.
② Cindy walk her dog everyday.
③ Can Sally plays the piano?
④ Janet must be in her room.
⑤ Let's eat out, will you?

**2.** 어법상 틀린 문장을 고르시오.

① You and I are too young.
② You can sit here.
③ This window won't shut.
④ It might snows tomorrow.
⑤ There must be some misunderstanding.

**3.** 문장 안에서 can의 쓰임이 <u>다른</u> 하나는?

① You <u>can</u> park here.
② <u>Can</u> I use the phone?
③ You <u>can't</u> go in.
④ <u>Can</u> you speak English?
⑤ We <u>can</u> swim here.

**4.** 문장 안에서 must의 쓰임이 <u>다른</u> 하나는?

① You must be tired.
② It must be true.
③ There must be something to eat in the fridge.
④ Your coat must be in the closet.
⑤ You must not make a U-turn here.

**5.** 문장의 부정문이 틀린 것은?

① I can ski. → I can't ski.
② You may park here. → You may not park here.
③ I will have dinner. → I won't have dinner.
④ She must be a student. → She may not be a student.
⑤ You have to wait for me. → You don't have to wait for me.

**6.** 밑줄 부분이 틀린 것은?

① <u>Have I</u> to pay extra for delivery?
② <u>Must you</u> watch television all day?
③ <u>Shall we</u> talk about it now?
④ <u>Can I</u> ask a question?
⑤ <u>Would you</u> pass me the salt?

**7.** 다음 글을 읽고 밑줄 친 문장을 해석하시오.

Korean people like instant noodles very much. Instant noodles called ramen are popular worldwide. Do you know how much they love these noodles? In Korean stores, you can buy more than 100 kinds of ramen. You can find beef, vegetable, chicken, squid and spicy or plain ramen. You can also find thick or thin ramen.

Whatever kind of ramen you like to eat, <u>they must have it</u> in Korea

*instant:인스턴트의, 즉석의 *squid:오징어
*spicy: 매운 *plain:순한

→

# *Chapter 5 | 시제

현재시제 | Unit 21
현재진행시제 | Unit 22
과거시제 | Unit 23
과거진행시제 | Unit 24
현재완료시제 | Unit 25
미래시제 | Unit 26

# 21 현재시제

**Grammar in Practice**

A: Tell me some things about your boyfriend.
B: He's good-looking and very kind to everyone.
He always **makes** others happy and **has** many friends.

---

**Grammar in Use**

**1.** 현재시제는 보통 다음과 같은 상황에서 쓴다.

● 지속적인 상태나 성질을 나타낼 때
I'm a 16-year-old girl. 나는 16살의 소녀다.
You **have** a good sense of humor. 너는 유머감각이 좋다.

● 반복적인 일이나 습관을 나타낼 때
We **have** a meeting every Monday. 우리는 월요일마다 회의를 한다.
Jack **drives** to work every day. Jack은 매일 직장에 차를 몰고 다닌다.

● 과학적이거나 일반적인 사실을 나타낼 때
Water **freezes** at 0℃. 물은 섭씨 0도에서 언다.
The sun **rises** in the east. 해는 동쪽에서 뜬다.

**2.** 주어가 3인칭 단수(she/ he/ it)일 때 동사에 -(e)s를 붙인다.

● 대부분의 동사는 -s를 붙인다.
come - come<u>s</u>      rain - rain<u>s</u>      eat - eat<u>s</u>      sleep - sleep<u>s</u>

● -s, -sh, -ch, -x로 끝나는 동사는 -es를 붙인다.
kiss - kiss<u>es</u>      brush - brush<u>es</u>      miss - miss<u>es</u>      mix - mix<u>es</u>

● 자음+y로 끝나는 동사는 y를 i로 바꾸고 -es를 붙인다.
study - stud<u>ies</u>      cry -cr<u>ies</u>      fly - fl<u>ies</u>      try - tr<u>ies</u>

● 불규칙동사가 있다.
have - <u>has</u>      do - <u>does</u>      go - <u>goes</u>

| 일반동사에 붙는 -(e)s의 발음 | | |
|---|---|---|
| 무성음(k, t, p, f등)뒤의 s | /s/ | helps, likes, wants, laughs 등 |
| -s, -sh, -ch, -x로 끝나는 동사 뒤의 -es | /iz/ | kisses, brushes, teaches, mixes 등 |
| 그 밖 유성음 뒤의 s | /z/ | plays, rains, snows, goes, studies 등 |

**3.** 일반동사를 포함한 현재형문장의 경우 부정문은 「주어+don't/doesn't+동사원형」, 의문문은 「Do/Does+주어+동사원형… ?」형태로 쓴다.

I **don't drink** Coke. 나는 콜라를 마시지 않는다.
Cindy **doesn't eat** pork. Cindy는 돼지고기를 먹지 않는다.
**Do** you **come** from the United States? 당신은 미국출신인가요?
**Does** Charles **teach** English? Charles는 영어를 가르치니?

# Unit Test

**1.** 다음 동사들을 3인칭 단수현재형으로 바꾸시오.

come → _____      go → _____      eat → _____

drink → _____     get → _____     take → _____

have → _____      dream → _____   sleep → _____

sit → _____       stand → _____   say → _____

pay → _____       buy → _____     cry → _____

**2.** 밑줄 친 곳이 어떻게 소리 나는지 알맞은 발음에 O표 하시오.

|          | /s/ | /z/ | /iz/ |
|----------|-----|-----|------|
| eats     |     |     |      |
| likes    |     |     |      |
| comes    |     |     |      |
| kisses   |     |     |      |
| sleeps   |     |     |      |
| buys     |     |     |      |
| finishes |     |     |      |
| goes     |     |     |      |
| wants    |     |     |      |
| listens  |     |     |      |

**3.** 괄호 안의 동사를 알맞은 형태로 바꾸어 빈칸을 채우시오.

Mr. Kim _____ (speak) English very well.  He _____ (take) a conversation class in the morning. After class, he _____ (listen) to an English tape on the way to work. He _____ (work) at a foreign bank, so he _____ (have) many chances to practice English at work. At home, he _____ (practice) English with his wife. His wife _____ (speak) English very well, too. This is how he _____ (study) English.

**4.** 우리말과 일치하도록 괄호 안의 단어를 알맞게 배열하시오.

1. Mark는 5개 언어를 말해요. (five/ speaks/ Mark/ languages)

   _____

2. 물은 100에 끓어요. (boils/ water/ at 100℃)

   _____

3. 나는 학교에 걸어서 간다. (walk/ I/ to/ school)

   _____

4. 해는 서쪽으로 진다. (sets/ the sun/ in the west)

   _____

5. 너 영어 잘한다. (speak/ English/ you/ well)

   _____

# Writing Pattern Practice

**1.** 「I/You/We/They + 동사~」 '나는/너(희)는/우리는/그들은 …한다'

나는 일찍 일어난다.

나는 캐나다 출신이에요.(come from) _____

너는 돈이 많구나.(a lot of) _____

우리는 하와이에서 살아요. _____

우리는 같은 학교에 다녀요. _____

그들은 영어를 잘 말해요. _____

Tom과 Mary는 교회에 다녀요.(church) _____


**2.** 「I/You/We/They + don't + 동사~」 '나는/너(희)는/우리는/그들은 …하지 않는다'

나는 돈이 많이 없어.(much money) _____

나는 운동을 하지 않아. _____

너는 여자친구가 없구나. _____

너는 열심히 공부하지 않는구나. _____

우리는 고기 안 먹어. _____

우리는 일을 하지 않아. _____

그들은 캐나다 출신이 아니야. _____

우리 부모님은 한국에 사시지 않아. _____


**3.** 「She/He/It + 동사(e)s~」 '그녀는/그는/그것은 …한다'

Jane은 매일 샤워를 해.(take) _____

Jack은 매일 회사에 차 몰고 가.(drive to work) _____

물은 섭씨 0도에서 얼어요.(freeze) _____

물은 섭씨 100도에서 끓어요.(boil) _____

그 상점은 9시에 문을 열어. _____

해는 동쪽에서 떠요.(in the east) _____


**4.** 「She/He/It + doesn't 동사원형~ 」 '그녀는/그는/그것은 …하지 않는다'

Cindy는 돼지고기를 먹지 않아.(pork) _____

David은 운동을 하지 않아. _____

언니는 콜라를 마시지 않아.(coke) _____

하와이에는 눈이 오지 않아. _____

# 22 현재진행시제

**Grammar in Practice**

A: What are the people in your family doing now?
B: My father is drinking coffee. He likes coffee.
My mother is making an omelette for lunch.
She cooks very well. My brother is watching TV.
He watches TV a lot.

**Grammar in Use**

**1.** 현재진행시제는 '…하는 중이다' 라는 뜻으로 「be+동사~ing」형태로 쓴다.
I'm **taking** a shower. 나는 샤워 중이다.
My brother **is talking** on the phone. 남동생은 전화 통화 중이다.
My mother and I **are cleaning** the house. 엄마와 나는 집안 청소중이다.

**2.** 현재형과 혼동하지 않도록 주의한다. 현재형은 주로 습관적인 행동을 말하는 반면 현재진행형은 현재 진행 중인 동작을 나타낸다. [비교]
I **go** to school. 나는 학교에 다닌다. I'm **going** to school. 나는 학교에 가고 있다.
Jim **smokes**. Jim은 담배를 핀다. Jim is **smoking**. Jim은 담배를 피고 있다.
We **eat** breakfast. 우리는 아침을 (보통) 먹는다. We**'re eating** breakfast. 우리는 아침을 먹고 있다.

**3.** 「동사~ing」 '현재분사' 를 만드는 규칙은 다음과 같다.
- 대부분의 동사는 동사원형에 -ing를 붙인다.
sleep - sleeping    read - reading    eat - eating
- -e로 끝나는 동사는 -e를 없애고 -ing를 붙인다.
live - living    come - coming    have - having
- 단모음+단자음으로 끝나는 동사는 자음을 하나 더 쓰고 -ing를 붙인다.
begin - beginning    prefer - preferring    control - controlling
- 2음절어인 경우 앞에 강세가 있으면 -ing만 붙인다.
open - opening    bother - bothering
- -ie로 끝나는 동사는 -ie를 y로 바꾸고 -ing를 붙인다.
lie - lying    tie - tying    die - dying

**4.** 부정문은 be동사 뒤에 not을 붙이고 의문문은 「Be동사+주어+동사~ing?」형태로 쓴다.
I'm **not sleeping**. 나는 자고 있지 않다.
Terry **isn't cleaning** his room. Terry는 방을 치우고 있지 않다.
**Am** I **bothering** you? 내가 너를 방해하고 있니?
**Are** you **eating** breakfast? 너는 아침 먹고 있니?
**Is** Monica **listening** to the radio? Monica는 라디오를 듣고 있니?

# Unit Test

**1.** 다음 동사의 현재 진행형을 쓰시오.

vacuum → _____     cry → _____     snow → _____

live → _____     go → _____     stop → _____

swim → _____     open → _____     rain → _____

die → _____     begin → _____     play → _____

**2.** 그림을 보고 보기의 표현을 이용하여 질문에 알맞게 답하시오.

보기 | eat some ice cream,  walk the dog,  sing,  play badminton,  take some pictures

1. What's Philip doing? He _____

2. What's Sarah doing? She _____

3. What's Ted doing? He _____

4. What's Ally doing? She _____

5. What are Jack and Julie doing? They _____

**3.** 괄호 안의 단어를 이용하여 현재형 또는 현재 진행형으로 빈칸을 채우시오.

1. What is Sue doing? _____ (she/ take a shower)

2. _____ (Cindy/ like coffee)  She drinks three cups of coffee a day.

3. You can turn off the TV. _____ (I/ not/ watch it/ now)

4. _____ (I/ look for/ my bag) Where is it?

5. Tim likes soccer. _____ (He/ play soccer/ very often)

96

# Writing Pattern Practice

**1.** 「주어 + be동사(am/are/is) + ~ing」 '나는 …하고 있다'

나는 샤워 중이야.(take a shower) _____

나는 학교에 가고 있어. _____

남동생은 전화 통화 중이야.(talk on the phone) _____

Jim은 담배를 피고 있어. _____

눈이 오고 있어. _____

해가 비추고 있어.(shine) _____

엄마와 나는 집안 청소중이야. _____

우리는 아침을 먹고 있어. _____

그들은 배드민턴을 치고 있어. _____


**2.** 「주어 + be동사(am/are/is) + not + ~ing」 '나는 …하고 있지 않다'

나는 자고 있지 않아. _____

나는 전화통화하고 있지 않아.(talk on the phone) _____

너는 숙제를 하고 있지 않구나. _____

너는 운동하고 있지 않구나. _____

Terry는 방을 치우고 있지 않아. _____

Kathy는 남동생을 괴롭히고 있지 않아. _____

비가 오고 있지 않아. _____

그들은 파티를 하고 있지 않아. _____


**3.** 「Be동사(am/are/is) + 주어 + ~ing?」 '내가 …하고 있니?'

내가 너를 방해를 하고 있니?(bother) _____

너는 아침 먹고 있니? _____

너는 샤워하고 있니?(take) _____

Monica는 라디오를 듣고 있니?(listen to) _____

John은 TV를 보고 있니? _____

비가 오고 있니? _____

그들은 바닥을 쓸고 있니?(sweep) _____

그들은 싸우고 있니?(fight) _____

Unit

# 23 | 과거시제

Grammar
in
Practice

A: How was your holiday?
B: It was very good.
A: What did you do?
B: I went to Cheju Island with my family.
　We went to the beach, and it was a lot of fun.

Grammar
in
Use

**1.** 과거시제는 이미 끝난 과거 행동이나 상태를 나타낸다.
Liz **went** shopping. Liz는 쇼핑 갔다.
She **was** with her friends. 그녀는 친구와 함께 있었다.
She **bought** a new coat. 그녀는 새 코트를 샀다.
It **was** kind of expensive. 그것은 약간 비쌌다.
She **liked** it very much. 그녀는 그것을 매우 마음에 들어 했다.

**2.** 동사의 과거형을 만드는 법칙은 다음과 같다.
● 동사원형에 −ed를 붙인다.
open - open**ed**　　rain - rain**ed**
● −e로 끝난 동사는 −d만 붙인다.
like - like**d**　　love - love**d**　　live - live**d**
● 「자음+y」로 끝나는 동사는 −y를 i로 바꾸고 −ed를 붙인다.
study - stud**ied**　　cry - cr**ied**　　worry - worr**ied**
● 「단모음+단자음」으로 끝나는 동사는 마지막 자음을 한 번 더 쓰고 −ed를 붙인다.
stop - stop**ped**　　drop - drop**ped**　　hug - hug**ged**　　prefer - prefer**red**
|예외1| 2음절 이상의 단어 중 마지막 음절에 강세가 있지 않은 경우
　　　open −open**ed**　　happen − happen**ed**　　bother − bother**ed**
　　　visit − visit**ed**　　remember − remember**ed**
|예외2| −y, −w, −x로 끝나는 단어는 −ed만 붙인다.
　　　enjoy enjoy**ed**　　snow − snow**ed**　　vow − vow**ed**　　mix − mix**ed**

**3.** 동사의 과거형 −ed는 /t/, /id/, /d/ 중 하나로 발음된다.

| /t/ | 무성음 (p, k, f 등) 뒤 | helped, liked, hoped, helped, washed |
|---|---|---|
| /d/ | 유성음 (b, g, v와 모음들) 뒤 | loved, studied, tried, played, listened |
| /id/ | −d, −t로 끝나는 동사 | needed, ended, hated, wanted, waited |

**4.** 일반동사를 포함한 과거형문장의 경우 부정문은 「주어+did not(didn't)+동사원형」, 의문문은 「Did+주어+동사원형…?」 형태로 쓴다.
I **didn't have** lunch. 나는 점심을 안 먹었다.
**Did** you **do** your homework? 너는 숙제 했니?

# WRAP-UP | 불규칙동사

| 동사원형 | 과거형 | 과거분사 뜻 | 동사원형 | 과거형 | 과거분사 뜻 |
|---|---|---|---|---|---|
| be(is/am/are) | was(were) | been 이다, 있다 | hold | held | held 잡다 |
| become | became | become ~가 되다 | hurt | hurt | hurt 상처입히다 |
| begin | began | begun 시작하다 | keep | kept | kept 지속하다 |
| bite | bit | bitten(bit) 물다 | know | knew | known 알다 |
| blow | blew | blown 불다, 폭파하다 | leave | left | left 떠나다, 남겨두다 |
| break | broke | broken 깨다, 어기다 | lend | lent | lent 빌려주다 |
| bring | brought | brought 가져오다 | let | let | let 놓다, 시키다 |
| build | built | built 건설하다 | lose | lost | lost 지다, 잃다 |
| buy | bought | bought 사다 | make | made | made 만들다 |
| catch | caught | caught 잡다 | mean | meant | meant 의미하다 |
| choose | chose | chosen 선택하다 | meet | met | met 만나다 |
| come | came | come 오다 | see | saw | seen 보다 |
| cost | cost | cost 비용이 들다 | sell | sold | sold 팔다 |
| cut | cut | cut 자르다 | send | sent | sent 보내다 |
| deal | dealt | dealt 다루다, 거래하다 | shake | shook | shaken 흔들다 |
| dig | dug | dug 파다 | shut | shut | shut 닫다 |
| do | did | done 하다 | sing | sang | sung 노래하다 |
| dream | dreamed (dreamt) | dreamed 꿈꾸다 (dreamt) | sit | sat | sat 앉다 |
| drink | drank | drunk 마시다 | sleep | slept | slept 자다 |
| drive | drove | driven 운전하다 | speak | spoke | spoken 말하다 |
| eat | ate | eaten 먹다 | spend | spent | spent 보내다 |
| fall | fell | fallen 떨어지다 | spread | spread | spread 펼치다 |
| feel | felt | felt 느끼다 | stand | stood | stood 서다 |
| fight | fought | fought 싸우다 | steal | stole | stolen 훔치다 |
| find | found | found 찾다, 알다 | stick | stuck | stuck 찌르다 |
| fly | flew | flown 날다 | swim | swam | swum 수영하다 |
| forget | forgot | forgotten 잊다 | take | took | taken 잡다, 취하다 |
| forgive | forgave | forgiven 용서하다 | teach | taught | taught 가르치다 |
| freeze | froze | frozen 얼리다 | tear | tore | torn 찢다 |
| get | got | got(gotten) 얻다 | tell | told | told 말하다 |
| give | gave | given 주다 | think | thought | thought 생각하다 |
| go | went | gone 가다 | throw | threw | thrown 던지다 |
| grow | grew | grown 자라다, 키우다 | understand | understood | understood 이해하다 |
| have | had | had 갖다 | wake | woke | woken 깨다(깨우다) |
| hear | heard | heard 듣다 | wear | wore | worn 입다 |
| hide | hid | hidden 숨기다 | win | won | won 이기다 |
| hit | hit | hit 치다, 때리다 | write | wrote | written 쓰다 |

## Unit Test

**1.** 다음은 우리가 생활에서 매일 사용할 만한 동사들이다. 빈칸에 알맞은 과거형을 적으시오.

1. wake up 깨다 - _____
2. get up 일어나다 - _____
3. wash 씻다 - _____
4. brush 닦다/빗다 - _____
5. take off 벗다 - _____
6. eat 먹다 - _____
7. put on 입다 - _____
8. go 가다 - _____
9. study 공부하다 - _____
10. have 가지다/먹다 - _____
11. play 놀다 - _____
12. come 오다 - _____
13. drink 마시다 - _____
14. watch 지켜보다/(TV를) 보다 - _____
15. tell 얘기하다 - _____
16. sleep 자다 - _____

**2.** 다음 John의 Hawaii 여행에 관한 글을 읽고 주어진 동사의 과거형을 이용하여 글을 완성하시오.

I _____ (go) to Hawaii with my parents. We _____ (leave) Seoul at night and _____ (arrive) in Hawaii in the morning. We _____ (swim) in the ocean and _____ (watch) people surfing. There _____ (be) a lot of interesting things to see. We _____ (have) a really great time and _____ (come) back the day before yesterday. I wish I could live in Hawaii.

**3.** 보기의 단어를 이용하여 과거형 문장을 완성하시오.

| 보기 | work   eat   fly   snow   wash |
|------|--------------------------------|

1. Yesterday it _____ all day, so we went out and made a snowman.
2. I _____ my face and brushed my teeth.
3. Jack _____ to Chicago to have an important meeting.
4. We _____ some pizza and drank some Coke.
5. Toby _____ at a foreign bank from 1995 until this year.

**4.** Tom 같이 각자 어제 한 일을 적어보시오.

| 보기 | I met my friends. We had dinner and watched a movie. The movie was a little boring, but I liked being with my friends. |
|------|------------------------------------------------------------------------------------------------------------------------|

_____

_____

_____

# Writing Pattern Practice

**1.** 「주어 + was/were ~」 '나는 …이었다'

나는 친구와 함께 있었어. _____

너는 뚱뚱했었는데. _____

Daniel은 오늘 아침에 늦었어. _____

우리는 지난주 부산에 있었어. _____

**2.** 「주어 + wasn't/weren't ~」 '나는 …이 아니었다'

나는 어젯밤 Ted와 함께 있지 않았어. _____

너는 날씬하지 않았어.(thin) _____

David은 결석하지 않았어.(absent) _____

어제는 덥지 않았어. _____

그들은 여기에 있지 않았어. _____

**3.** 「Was/ were + 주어 ~ ?」 '내가 …이었니?'

내가 늦었었나? _____

너는 파티에 있었니? _____

어제는 화창했니?(sunny) _____

그들은 피곤해했니? _____

**4.** 「주어 + 과거동사~」 '나는 …했다'

나는 친구들과 영화를 봤어. _____

너 새 코트 샀구나. _____

Liz는 쇼핑 갔어. _____

우리는 숙제 했어. _____

부모님은 일본으로 떠나셨어.(leave for) _____

**5.** 「주어 + didn't +동사원형~」 '나는 …하지 않았다'

나는 숙제를 하지 않았어. _____

나는 어젯밤 잠을 잘 못 잤어. _____

너는 네 방을 치우지 않았구나. _____

비가 오지 않았어. _____

우리는 일찍 일어나지 않았어. _____

**6.** 「Did + 주어 + 동사원형~?」 '내가 …했니?'

내가 너를 방해했니?(bother) _____

내가 너를 깨웠니?(wake) _____

너는 이 닦았니? _____

Julia가 어젯밤 너에게 전화했니? _____

# 24 과거진행시제

 Grammar in Practice

Detective: What were you doing at 11 last night?
Suspect1 : I was driving home.
Suspect2 : I was sleeping.

---

 Grammar in Use

**1.** 과거진행시제는 과거의 어느 때에 일어나고 있었던 일을 말하며 '~하고 있었다'라는 뜻으로 「be동사의 과거형(was, were)+동사~ing」 형태로 쓴다.

I **was thinking** about you. 나는 당신 생각 하고 있었어요.
My brother **was taking** a shower. 남동생은 샤워하고 있었다.
My friends and I **were having** a party. 친구들과 나는 파티를 하고 있었다.

**2.** 과거형과 혼동하지 않도록 비교해보면서 주의한다.

I helped my mother clean the house. (과거) 나는 엄마께 집안일을 도와드렸다.
I **was helping** my mother clean the house. (과거진행) 나는 엄마께 집안일을 도와드리고 있었다.

Molly ate pizza for lunch. (과거) Molly는 점심으로 피자를 먹었다.
Molly **was eating** pizza for lunch. (과거진행) Molly는 점심으로 피자를 먹고 있었다.

Jack vacuumed the floor. (과거) Jack은 바닥을 진공청소기로 청소했다.
Jack **was vacuuming** the floor. (과거진행) Jack은 바닥을 진공청소기로 청소하고 있었다.

**3.** 부정문은 be동사 뒤에 not을 붙이고 의문문은 「Be동사+주어+동사-ing?」 형태로 쓴다.

My father **was reading** a book. 아버지는 책을 읽고 계셨다.
We **were having** a house-warming party. 우리는 집들이를 하고 있었다.
**Were** you **talking** on the phone? 너는 전화통화하고 있었니?
**Was Mark taking** a shower? Mark는 샤워하고 있었니?

# Unit Test

**1.** 과거형 문장을 과거진행형 문장으로 고치시오.

1. I watched a movie. → _____

2. Jinny drove home. → _____

3. My uncle rode a horse. → _____

4. We did our homework. → _____

5. My daughter talked on the phone. → _____


**2.** Kelly의 오늘 한 일이다. 주어진 시간에 무슨 일을 하고 있었는지 과거진행형으로 쓰시오.

1.

7:30-8:00AM
have breakfast

2.

8:30-9:00AM
drive to work

3.

9:00AM-6:00PM
work

1. What was she doing at 7:40AM? She _____

2. What was she doing at 8:40AM? She _____

3. What was she doing at 5:00PM? She _____


**3.** 우리말과 일치하도록 괄호 안의 단어를 알맞게 배열하시오.

1. 나는 모자를 쓰고 있었다. (I/ wearing/ was/ a hat)

_____

2. 그 소녀는 아이스크림을 먹고 있었다. (ice cream/ the girl/ was/ eating)

_____

3. 비가 오고 있었다. (was/ it/ raining)

_____

4. 우리는 이탈리아에 살고 있었다. (in Italy/ were/ we/ living)

_____

5. Leo와 나는 테니스를 치고 있었다. (were/ Leo and I/ playing/ tennis)

_____

# Writing Pattern Practice

**1.** 「I was + ~ing」 '나는 …하고 있었다'

나는 너 생각 하고 있었어.(think about)

나는 모자를 쓰고 있었어.(wear)

너는 자고 있었구나.

Molly는 점심으로 피자를 먹고 있었어.(for lunch)

내 친구들과 나는 파티를 하고 있었어.

Jack은 바닥을 진공청소기로 청소하고 있었어.(vacuum)

Leo와 나는 테니스를 치고 있었어.

눈이 오고 있었어.


**2.** 「I wasn't + ~ing」 '나는 …하고 있지 않았다'

나는 공부하고 있지 않았어.

나는 시험에 대한 생각을 하고 있지 않았어.

너는 운동하고 있지 않았구나.(exercise)

Tom은 방을 치우고 있지 않았어.

Kate는 남동생을 괴롭히고 있지 않았어.(bother)

그들은 파티를 하고 있지 않았어.

그들은 너를 기다리고 있지 않았어.


**3.** 「Was I + ~ing?」 '내가 …하고 있었니?'

너는 아침 먹고 있었니?

너는 샤워하고 있었니?(take)

너는 이 펜을 찾고 있었니?(look for)

Monica는 라디오를 듣고 있었니?(listen to)

Jack은 TV를 보고 있었니?

그 소녀는 아이스크림을 먹고 있었니?

비가 오고 있었니?

그들은 싸우고 있었니?(fight)

## Unit 25 현재완료시제

**Grammar in Practice**

A: Have you ever been to Disneyland?

B: No, but I have seen some pictures of it. Is it really big?

A: Yes, it took our family a whole week to see everything.

**Grammar in Use**

**1.** 과거형문장이 '~을 했다'인 반면 현재완료문장은 '과거의 어떤 일로 인해 현재 어떠하다' 라는 의미로 쓴다. 형태는 「주어+have/has+과거분사」이며 과거의 특정한 시점을 나타내는 부사 (yesterday, last Friday, last night 등)와 같이 쓰지 않는다.

I can't have lunch with you now.

| I've already had lunch. |
| --- |

과거                                                     현재

**2.** '지금 막 ~했다' 라는 완료의 의미로 쓴다.

I**'ve just had** dinner. 나는 금방 저녁을 먹었어. (just: '막 ~했다')

I**'ve already finished** my homework. 나는 이미 숙제를 끝마쳤다. (already: '이미~했다')

A: Are you ready to order? 주문하시겠어요?

B: Sorry, I **haven't decided yet**. 미안해요. 아직 결정 못했어요. (부정문의 yet: '아직~하지 않았다')

A: **Have** Tom and Mary **arrived yet**? Tom과 Mary가 도착했어?

B: No, not yet. 아니, 아직 안했어. (의문문의 yet: 어떤 일이 지금쯤 일어났을 것으로 기대할 때 쓴다.)

**3.** '~해본 적이 있다' 라는 경험의 의미로 쓴다.

A: **Have** you ever **been** to Florida? Florida에 가본 적 있어?

B: Yes, I have. 응, 있어.

**4.** '계속 ~해왔다' 라는 계속의 의미로 쓴다. 「How long+have/has+주어+과거분사?」의 형태로 '얼마나 오래 ~해왔니?' 라는 질문을 많이 한다.

A: **How long have you known** each other? 너희는 얼마나 알고 지냈니?

B: We**'ve known** each other for 10 years. 우리는 10년 동안 알고 지냈어.

**5.** '~해버려서 지금은 …이다' 라는 결과의 의미로 쓴다.

She **has left** for New York. (So she is not here.) 그녀는 뉴욕으로 떠나 버렸다.

A: Would you like some more? 더 먹을래?

B: No, thanks. I**'ve had** enough. (So I'm full now.) 아니 고맙지만 됐어. 충분히 먹었어.

# Unit Test

**1.** 괄호안의 표현을 이용하여 현재완료시제 문장을 완성하시오.

1. I _____ (just finish) my work.
2. I _____ (be) busy.
3. Peter _____ (wait for you) for an hour.
4. I _____ (turn off) the computer.
5. It _____ (rain) for a week.
6. My friends and I _____ (be) to Hawaii once.
7. Heather _____ (try) bungy jumping.
8. Jimmy _____ (get) a new job.
9. We _____ (know) each other since 2000.
10. It _____ (be cold) since then.

**2.** 그림을 보고 괄호 안의 단어를 이용하여, 현재완료시제 문장을 만드시오.

two hours ago          now

1.

1. (leave home)
She _____

2.

2. (buy glasses)
He _____

3.

3. (break his leg)
He _____

**3.** 문장이 맞았으면 T(True), 틀렸으면 F(False)라고 쓰고 틀린 곳을 고쳐 쓰시오.

1. I slept well. I feel great.
2. The movie has begun at 3 o'clock.
3. We've finished the work yesterday.
4. It has rained for a couple of days.
5. Jane and I have known each other for a long time.

106

# Writing Pattern Practice

**1.** 「주어 + have/has + 과거분사」 '나는 막 …했다' → 완료

나는 금방 저녁을 먹었어.(have) _____

나는 이미 숙제를 끝마쳤어.(already) _____

Jane은 금방 떠났어. _____

나는 아직 결정 못했어. _____

너는 막 집에 도착했니?(get) _____

Cindy는 벌써 떠났니?(already) _____

**2.** 「주어 + have/has + 과거분사」 '나는 …해본 적이 있다' → 경험

나는 멕시코 음식을 먹어본 적이 있어.(try, Mexican food) _____

너는 영화 Titanic을 본적이 있구나.(the movie 'Titanic') _____

우리는 디즈니랜드에 가본 적이 있어.(Disneyland) _____

James는 번지점핑을 해본 적이 없어.(try bungy jumping) _____

너는 플로리다에 가본 적 있니?(Florida) _____

**3.** 「주어 + have/has + 과거분사」 '나는 계속 …해왔다' → 계속

나는 너를 1시간동안 기다렸어. _____

Ted는 20년 동안 여기에서 일해 왔어. _____

일주일동안 비가 왔다. _____

우리는 10년 동안 알아왔어. _____

우리는 Mr. Kim을 1년 동안 못 봤어. _____

비가 얼마나 오래왔지? _____

너희는 얼마나 오래 서로 알고 지냈니? _____

**4.** 「주어 + have/has + 과거분사」 '나는 ~해버려서 지금은 …이다' → 결과

나는 충분히 먹었어.(have enough) _____

나는 내 책을 잃어 버렸어. _____

Janet은 미국에 가 있어.(go) _____

Nancy는 뉴욕으로 떠나 버렸어.(leave for) _____

너는 숙제를 마쳤니? _____

# 26 미래시제

A: I'm going to have a birthday party this Friday.
   Will you come?
B: Sure. I will.
A: Good. Jack and Michael are coming, too.

---

**1.** 「will+동사원형」은 '~을 할 것이다' 라는 뜻으로 미래시제를 나타낸다.
   I **will** be in Chicago next week. 나는 다음 주에 시카고에 갈 거야.
   **Will** you be on time? 정시에 올 거야?

**2.** will의 부정은 will not이며 won't로 축약할 수 있다.
   Mom, I **won't** let you down. 엄마, 실망시켜 드리지 않을게요.
   **Won't** you help me get up? 나 일어나는거 안 도와줄래?

**3.** 「be going to+동사원형」은 '~을 할 예정이다' 라는 뜻으로 미래시제를 나타낸다.
   We're **going** to see a movie tonight. 우리는 오늘밤 영화를 보러갈 예정이야.
   **Is** it **going to** rain? 비가 올까?

**4.** be going to의 부정은 be동사 뒤에 not을 붙인다.
   I'm **not going to** have dinner. I'm on a diet. 저녁 안 먹을 거야. 다이어트 중이거든.
   It's **not going to** snow much. 눈이 많이 오지 않을 예정이다.

**5.** 확실하고 가까운 미래를 나타낼 때는 「be+동사~ing」를 쓰기도 한다.
   I'm **leaving** tonight. 나 오늘밤 떠나.
   Kate **is getting** married next week. Kate는 다음 주에 결혼해.

# Unit Test

**1.** 그림을 be going to를 사용하여 설명하시오.

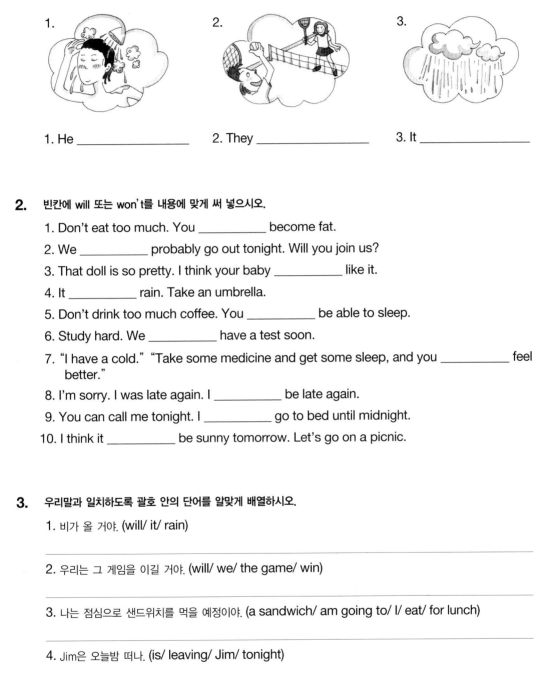

1. He _____

2. They _____

3. It _____

**2.** 빈칸에 will 또는 won't를 내용에 맞게 써 넣으시오.

1. Don't eat too much. You _____ become fat.

2. We _____ probably go out tonight. Will you join us?

3. That doll is so pretty. I think your baby _____ like it.

4. It _____ rain. Take an umbrella.

5. Don't drink too much coffee. You _____ be able to sleep.

6. Study hard. We _____ have a test soon.

7. "I have a cold." "Take some medicine and get some sleep, and you _____ feel better."

8. I'm sorry. I was late again. I _____ be late again.

9. You can call me tonight. I _____ go to bed until midnight.

10. I think it _____ be sunny tomorrow. Let's go on a picnic.

**3.** 우리말과 일치하도록 괄호 안의 단어를 알맞게 배열하시오.

1. 비가 올 거야. (will/ it/ rain)

_____

2. 우리는 그 게임을 이길 거야. (will/ we/ the game/ win)

_____

3. 나는 점심으로 샌드위치를 먹을 예정이야. (a sandwich/ am going to/ I/ eat/ for lunch)

_____

4. Jim은 오늘밤 떠나. (is/ leaving/ Jim/ tonight)

_____

5. 우리는 그 파티에 안가요. (going/ the party/ we/ aren't/ to)

_____

# Writing Pattern Practice

**1.** 「I will +동사원형」 '나는 …할 거야'

나는 다음주에 시카고에 갈 거야.(Chicago) _____

나는 너를 그리워할 거야.(miss) _____

엄마, 제가 실망시켜 드리지 않을게요. _____

너 뚱뚱해질 거야.(be) _____

화창할거야.(sunny) _____

우리는 그 게임을 이길 거야. _____

너는 무엇을 할 거니? _____

너는 정시에 올 거니?(on time) _____

너 우리와 함께할래?(join us) _____

나 일어나는거 안 도와줄래?(help me get up) _____


**2.** 「I'm going to + 동사원형」 '나는 …할 예정이야'

나는 수영할 예정이야. _____

나는 저녁 안 먹을 거야. _____

우리는 오늘밤 영화를 보러갈 예정이야. _____

숙모가 아기를 가졌어요.(have a baby) _____

너는 무엇을 할 예정이니? _____

너는 집에 있을 예정이니?(be) _____

비가 올까? _____


**3.** 「I'm + 동사~ing」 '나는 …해'

나 오늘밤 떠나.(tonight) _____

Kate는 다음 주에 결혼해. _____

David은 1시간 후에 여기 도착해.(get) _____

우리는 그 파티에 안가. _____

너는 오늘밤 뭐하니? _____

너 오늘밤 오니? _____

# WRAP-UP | 시제

| 시제 | 긍정문 | 부정문 | 의문문 |
|---|---|---|---|
| 현재 | 「주어+동사/동사(e)s」<br>You exercise.<br>Sue gets up early. | 「주어+don't/doesn't+동사원형」<br>You don't exercise.<br>Sue doesn't get up early. | 「Do/Does+주어+동사원형?」<br>Do you exercise?<br>Does Sue get up early? |
| 현재진행 | 「주어+be동사+동사─ing」<br>You're studying.<br>Sue is watching TV. | 「주어+be동사+not+동사─ing」<br>You aren't studying.<br>Sue isn't watching TV. | 「Be동사+주어+동사─ing?」<br>Are you studying?<br>Is Sue watching TV? |
| 과거 | 「주어+과거동사」<br>You did your homework.<br>Sue went out for lunch. | 「주어+didn't+동사원형」<br>You didn't do your homework.<br>Sue didn't go out for lunch. | 「Did+주어+동사원형?」<br>Did you do your homework?<br>Did Sue go out for lunch? |
| 과거진행 | 「주어+be동사(과거)+동사─ing」<br><br>You were sleeping.<br>Sue was having dinner. | 「주어+be동사(과거)+not+동사─ing」<br><br>You weren't sleeping.<br>Sue wasn't having dinner. | 「Be동사(과거)+주어+동사─ing?」<br>Were you sleeping?<br>Was Sue having dinner? |
| 현재완료 | 「주어+have/has+과거분사」<br><br>You've been to Disneyland.<br>Sue has tried skydiving. | 「주어+have/has not<br>(haven't/ hasn't)+과거분사」<br>You haven't been to Disneyland.<br>Sue hasn't tried skydiving. | 「Have/Has+주어+과거분사?」<br><br>Have you been to Disneyland?<br>Has Sue tried skydiving? |
| 미래 | 「주어+will+동사원형」<br>You'll be late.<br>Sue will see a movie.<br><br>「주어+be going to+동사원형」<br><br>You're going to be absent.<br>Sue is going to have a party.<br><br>「주어+be동사+동사─ing」<br>You're going to Hawaii.<br>Sue is leaving tonight. | 「주어+will not(won't)+동사원형」<br>You won't be late.<br>Sue won't see a movie.<br><br>「주어+be not going to+동사원형」<br><br>You aren't going to be absent.<br>Sue isn't going to have a party.<br><br>「주어+be동사+not+동사─ing」<br>You aren't going to Hawaii.<br>Sue isn't leaving tonight. | 「Will+주어+동사원형?」<br>Will you be late?<br>Will Sue see a movie?<br><br>「Be동사+주어+ going to<br>+동사원형?」<br>Are you going to be absent?<br>Is Sue going to have a party?<br><br>「Be동사+주어+동사─ing?」<br>Are You going to Hawaii?<br>Is Sue leaving tonight? |

**1.** 다음 문장을 영어로 쓰시오.

① 그는 매일 운동한다.　　　　　　　　　　　→ _____

② 나는 저녁 먹었어.　　　　　　　　　　　　→ _____

③ 우리는 Thai 음식을 먹어본 적이 없어.　　　→ _____

④ 비가 올까?(will)　　　　　　　　　　　　　→ _____

⑤ 너희는 파티를 할 예정이니?(be going to)　→ _____

**2.** 다음 문장을 우리말로 쓰시오.

① You were fat.　　　　　　　　　→ _____

② Were you sleeping?　　　　　　→ _____

③ Have you ever been to Paris?　→ _____

④ I've just arrived here.　　　　　→ _____

⑤ Is it going to snow?　　　　　　→ _____

**3.** 다음 중 틀린 곳을 바르게 고치시오.

① I'm take a shower now.　　　　_____

② Did you your homework?　　　_____

③ I was watch TV.　　　　　　　_____

④ Will Jane sees a movie?　　　　_____

⑤ Have you ever be there?　　　_____

**4.** 문장을 괄호 안의 지시대로 바꾸시오.

① Sue gets up early. (의문문으로)　　　　　→ _____

② I lost my keys. (부정문으로)　　　　　　　→ _____

③ We didn't take a vacation. (긍정문)　　　→ _____

④ Has Jane had lunch? (평서문으로)　　　　→ _____

⑤ Shakespeare wrote many plays. (의문문으로)　→ _____

⑥ I'll go to bed early. (부정문으로)　　　　　→ _____

⑦ They're going to invite Karen. (의문문으로)　→ _____

⑧ I haven't told him. (긍정문으로)　　　　　→ _____

⑨ Is it going to rain? (평서문으로)　　　　　→ _____

⑩ I've started my new job. (부정문으로)　　→ _____

**1.** 어법상 맞는 문장을 고르시오.

① What time is Mary arrive?

② I've just brushed my teeth.

③ Has Alice buy a new computer yet?

④ We're still wait for you.

⑤ Every morning the sun is rising in the east.

**2.** 시제가 잘못 쓰인 문장을 고르시오.

① I go shopping every weekend.

② We will see a movie next Friday.

③ We went out last night.

④ My family is eating out last Sunday.

⑤ Lauren has waited for you for an hour.

**3.** 괄호 안 동사의 알맞은 형태를 고르시오.

> 보기 | Next week she ( be ) in New York.

① will be          ② is

③ was             ④ be

⑤ being

[4–5] 괄호 안에 들어갈 수 있는 말을 고르시오.

**4.** Amy _____ to the movies twice last week.

① to go

② will go

③ goes

④ has gone

⑤ went

**5.** Have you _____ Richard, or should I introduce you?

① meet

② met

③ will meet

④ to meet

⑤ meeting

**6.** 빈칸에 들어갈 알맞은 문장을 고르시오.

> 보기 | A: _____
> B: I was talking on the phone.

① What do you do?

② What did you do?

③ What will you do?

④ What were you doing?

⑤ What are you doing?

**7.** 다음 글을 읽고 괄호 안에 들어갈 동사가 알맞게 짝 지어진 것을 고르시오

① celebrate - pick

② celebrated - picked

③ will celebrate - pick

④ celebrated - pick

⑤ celebrate - will pick

 During Valentine's Day, on February 14th, most of the world celebrates love. In Rome, young men and women _____ love two thousand years ago. However, they didn't give each other cards, flowers, or chocolates. The women put their names in an urn. Then the men _____ a name out of the urn and he had to be that woman's boyfriend for one year. Thank goodness we don't do that anymore.

*urn: 단지

# * Chapter 6 | 부정사와 동명사

명사 역할을 하는 to 부정사 | Unit 27

형용사 역할을 하는 to 부정사 | Unit 28

부사 역할을 하는 to 부정사 | Unit 29

to 부정사의 의미상 주어 | Unit 30

to 부정사를 이용한 다양한 표현 | Unit 31

동명사의 역할 | Unit 32

목적어로 쓰이는 부정사와 동명사 | Unit 33

# 27 | 명사 역할을 하는 to부정사

**Grammar in Practice**

A: What do you want to do?
B: I want to play tennis.
A: It's a little cold outside. Why don't we just play table tennis inside?
B: That sounds OK.

**Grammar in Use**

**1.** 부정사란 보통 동사원형을 말하므로 to 부정사의 형태는 「to+동사원형」이다. to 부정사는 동사가 문장 안에서 명사(~하는 것), 형용사(~의, ~하는), 부사(~하기 위해서, ~ 때문에 등) 역할을 할 때 쓴다.

I want **to go** bowling. (명사 역할) 나는 볼링 치러 가는 것을 원한다.
I need something **to eat**. (형용사 역할) 나는 먹을 것을 필요로 한다.
I came **to see** you. (부사 역할) 너를 보러 왔다.
I decided **not to go** out. 나는 나가지 않기로 결정했다.

**| MORE TIPS |** to 부정사의 부정은 「not to+동사원형」이다.

**2.** 「to+동사원형」이 명사역할을 할 때 일반 명사와 같이 문장에서 주어, 목적어, 보어 역할을 한다. 전치사의 목적어 역할은 하지 않는다.

● **주어 역할 :** to 부정사가 주어자리에 올 경우 주로 가짜주어 it을 쓰고 진짜 주어는 뒤로 보낸다.
**To be with my friends** is fun. → It's fun **to be with my friends**.
친구들과 함께 있는 것은 즐겁다.

**To exercise every day** is important. → It's important **to exercise every day**.
매일 운동하는 것은 중요하다.

**To get there on time** is impossible. → It's impossible **to get there on time**.
거기에 정각에 도착하기란 불가능하다.

● **목적어 역할**
Tess needs **to clean** her room. Tess는 방을 치울 필요가 있다.
"What would you like **to eat**?" 무엇을 먹고 싶어요?
"I'd like **to eat** spaghetti." 나는 스파게티를 먹고 싶어요.

**| MORE TIPS |** 모든 동사가 to부정사를 목적어로 가질 수 있는 것은 아니다.

● **보어역할**
My goal is **to be** a doctor. (주격보어) 내 목표는 의사가 되는 것이다.
My plan is **to lose** ten kilograms a month. (주격보어) 내 계획은 한 달에 10kg을 빼는 것이다.
I want you **to come** to my party. (목적격보어) 네가 내 파티에 왔으면 좋겠어.
I told you **to come** on time. (목적격보어) 내가 너한테 정각에 오라고 말했잖아.

# Unit Test

**1.** 주어진 동사를 이용하여 to~ 또는 not to ~ 형태로 빈칸에 써 넣으시오.

1. "What would you like to do?" "I'd like _____ a movie." (see)
2. I tried _____ late. (be)
3. I'm very tired. I need _____ in bed. (stay)
4. Where's Abby? She promised _____ here by six. (be)
5. We can't go on a picnic. It started _____ (rain)
6. I don't have enough money. I decided _____ to Europe. (travel)
7. I tried _____ my homework, but I was too tired. (do)
8. I have to go right now. I hate _____ (be) late.
9. Jason seems _____ (be) healthy. He rarely catches a cold.
10. You're a good driver. When did you learn _____ ? (drive)

**2.** 보기에서 가장 적당한 말을 골라 빈칸에 써 넣으시오.

| 보기 | to eat,   to be,   to turn off,   to ask,   to drive |
| --- | --- |

1. I want _____ a sandwich.
2. You have a car. When did you learn _____ ?
3. I need _____ you something.
4. I'd like _____ with you.
5. Jeff forgot _____ the light.

**3.** 우리말과 일치하도록 괄호 안의 단어를 알맞게 배열하시오.

1. 나는 차를 팔기로 결정했다. (I/ to/ sell/ decided/ my car)

   _____

2. 너는 무엇을 하기를 원하니? (do/ want/ you/ what/ do/ to/ ?)

   _____

3. 나는 최선을 다하기 위해 노력했다. (to/ tried/ do/ I/ my best)

   _____

4. 나는 늦기 싫다. (I/ to/ hate/ late/ be)

   _____

5. Jane은 Italy로 가기로 결심했다. (to Italy/ decided/ Jane/ to/ go)

   _____

6. 당신은 샌드위치 드실래요? (a sandwich/ you/ to/ would/ like/ eat/ ?)

   _____

7. Rita는 가수가 되기를 희망한다. (hopes/ to/ Rita/ a singer/ be)

   _____

# Writing Pattern Practice _「to+동사원형」: 명사

**1. 주어 역할 '…하는 것은'**

내 친구들과 함께 있는 것은 즐겁다.(fun) _____

영어를 배우는 것은 신난다.(exciting) _____

매일 운동하는 것은 중요하다. _____

스파게티를 만드는 것은 어렵다.(difficult) _____

여기서 택시를 잡는 것은 쉽지 않다.(catch a taxi) _____

담배를 끊는 것은 어렵다.(hard, quit) _____

거기에 정각에 도착하기란 불가능하다.(get) _____

**2. 목적어 역할 '…하는 것을'**

나는 볼링 치러 가는 것을 원한다.(go bowling) _____

Tess는 방을 치울 필요가 있다. _____

Jane은 떠나지 않기로 결정했다. _____

Rita는 가수가 되기를 희망한다. _____

나는 스파게티를 먹고 싶어요.('d like) _____

불을 끄는 것을 잊지 마.(turn off) _____

비가 오기 시작했다.(start) _____

나는 외식하는 것을 좋아한다. _____

Jane은 방 치우는 것을 싫어한다. _____

나는 최선을 다하기 위해 노력했다.(do) _____

당신은 샌드위치 드실래요?(Would you like~) _____

**3. 보어 역할 '…하는 것이다'**

내 꿈은 의사가 되는 것이다.(become) _____

나는 네가 내 파티에 왔으면 좋겠어. _____

너는 내가 가수가 되었으면 좋겠어? _____

내가 너한테 정각에 오라고 말했잖아. _____

엄마는 항상 나에게 공부 열심히 하라고 말씀하신다. _____

# Unit 28 | 형용사 역할을 하는 to부정사

**Grammar in Practice**

A: I'm thirsty.
B: I'll get you something to drink. What would you like?
A: I'd like some water.
B: Here you are.

**Grammar in Use**

1. 「to+동사원형」이 형용사 역할을 할 때는 수식하는 명사 뒤에 쓴다.

- 할 일: something to do
  I have **something to do**. 나는 할 일이 있다.

- 먹을 음식: food to eat
  There is no **food to eat**. 먹을 음식이 없다.

- 쓸 돈: money to spend
  He has a lot of **money to spend**. 그는 쓸 돈이 많이 있다.

- 만날 친구들: friends to meet
  I have some **friends to meet** today. 나는 오늘 만날 친구들이 좀 있다.

- 마실 물: water to drink
  Give me some **water to drink**. 마실 물 좀 줘.

2. 수식 받는 명사가 전치사의 목적어인 경우, to 부정사 뒤에 전치사를 쓴다.

- 앉을 의자: a chair to sit on
  There are no **chairs to sit on**. 앉을 의자가 없다.

- 점심 같이 먹을 친구: a friend to have lunch with
  I want **a friend to have lunch with**. 나는 점심 같이 먹을 친구가 필요하다.

- 쓸 것(필기도구): something to write with
  I need **something to write with**. 나는 쓸 것이 필요하다.

- 쓸 것(종이): something to write on
  Please give me **something to write on**. 쓸 종이 좀 주세요.

- 말할 누군가: someone to talk to
  I need **someone to talk to**. 나는 말할 누군가가 필요하다.

# Unit Test

**1.** 밑줄 친 to 부정사가 형용사적으로 쓰였으면 '형용사', 명사적으로 쓰였으면 '명사' 라고 적으시오.

1. I want <u>to be</u> a doctor. (　　　)
2. It's important <u>to exercise</u> every day. (　　　)
3. Do you want me <u>to check again</u>? (　　　)
4. I'll get you something <u>to write with</u>. (　　　)
5. I don't have enough time <u>to finish</u> it. (　　　)
6. Here is a chair <u>to sit on</u>. (　　　)
7. I need a friend <u>to talk to</u>. (　　　)
8. That man has no house <u>to live in</u>. (　　　)
9. It has started <u>to rain</u>. (　　　)
10. I decided not <u>to study</u> abroad. (　　　)
11. I'd love <u>to go</u> to Prague. (　　　)
12. Jane hates <u>to be</u> late to class. (　　　)
13. It's impossible <u>to lose</u> 10kg in a week. (　　　)
14. Did you decide <u>to sell</u> your house? (　　　)
15. You have a lot of homework <u>to do</u>. (　　　)

**2.** 우리말과 일치하도록 괄호 안의 단어를 알맞게 배열하시오.

1. 나는 먹을 것이 필요하다. (need/ I/ eat/ something/ to)

_____

2. 너는 할 일이 많구나. (have/ you/ to/ a lot of/ do/ things)

_____

3. Jane은 읽을 책을 좀 샀다. (some books/ read/ bought/ Jane/ to)

_____

4. Bob은 잘 시간이 없다. (has/ no time/ Bob/ sleep/ to)

_____

5. 너는 의지할 친구가 필요해. (to/ need/ a friend/ you/ rely on)

_____

6. 우리는 점심 먹을 시간이 없었다. (no/ we/ to/ time/ have lunch/ had)

_____

7. 그들은 영화 볼 시간이 없었다. (time/ they/ no/ had/ to/ see a movie)

_____

8. 냉장고에 먹을 것이 있다. (something/ there is/ eat/ to/ in the fridge)

_____

9. 너는 끝내야할 숙제 있니? (finish/ have/ to/ any homework/ do you/ ?)

_____

10. 내가 너에게 마실 것을 가져다줄게. (something/ get you/ to/ I'll/ drink)

_____

# Writing Pattern Practice _「to+동사원형」: 형용사

**1.** 「명사 + to부정사」

할 일

나는 할 일이 있다.

읽을 것

나는 읽을 것이 필요하다.

먹을 음식

먹을 음식이 없다.

쓸 돈

그는 쓸 돈이 많이 있다.

만날 친구들

나는 오늘 만날 친구들이 있다.

마실 물

내게 마실 물 좀 줘.

**2.** 「명사 + to부정사 + 전치사」

앉을 의자들

앉을 의자들이 없다.(no)

영어공부같이 하는 친구

나는 영어공부같이 하는 친구가 필요해.

점심 같이 먹을 친구

나는 점심 같이 먹을 친구가 필요하다.

쓸 것(필기도구)(something)

나는 쓸 것이 필요하다.

쓸 것(종이)

내게 쓸 종이 좀 주세요.(Please~)

말할 누군가(someone)

나는 말할 누군가가 필요하다.

살 집

너는 살 집이 있니?

같이 살 룸메이트

나는 같이 살 룸메이트를 원한다.

# 29 | 부사 역할을 하는 to부정사

**Grammar in Practice**

A: Nice to meet you.
B: Nice to meet you, too.
A: I've heard a lot about you.
B: Only good things, I hope.

---

**Grammar in Use**

**1.** 「to+동사원형」는 문장 안에서 부사 역할을 하여 동사나 형용사 등을 꾸며주기도 한다.

- 목적: ～하기 위해서, ～하려고
  I came here **to see** Henry. 나는 여기에 Henry보러 왔어요.
  He did his best **to win** the game. 그는 게임에서 이기기 위해 최선을 다했다.

- 원인: ～하니까, ～해서
  It's nice **to meet** you. 만나서 반가워요.
  I'm glad **to hear** that news. 그 소식을 들으니 기뻐.

- 이유, 판단의 근거: ～하다니, ～을 보니
  You were foolish **to do** something like that. 그런 행동을 하다니 너는 어리석었다.
  You must be a genius **to solve** the problem. 그 문제를 해결하다니 너는 천재임에 틀림없다.

- 결과: ～해서 …하다
  He grew up **to be** a great singer. 그는 자라서 훌륭한 가수가 되었다.
  Her mother lived **to be** eighty. 그녀의 어머니는 80세까지 사셨다.

- 형용사 수식: ～하기에
  This book was fun **to read**. 이 책은 읽기에 재미있었다.
  This river is very dangerous **to swim in**. 이 강은 수영하기에 매우 위험하다.

# Unit Test

**1.** 밑줄 친 to 부정사가 형용사적으로 쓰였으면 '형용사', 명사적으로 쓰였으면 '명사' 부사적으로 쓰였으면 '부사' 라고 적으시오.

1. I was pleased <u>to see</u> Kate. (　　　)
2. My father was very lucky <u>to get</u> a new job. (　　　)
3. I'm planning <u>to go</u> on a summer holiday. (　　　)
4. Can I get you something <u>to drink</u>? (　　　)
5. What would you like <u>to eat</u>? (　　　)
6. The children need some toys <u>to play with</u>. (　　　)
7. You were lucky <u>to get</u> there on time. (　　　)
8. Janet was so excited <u>to see</u> Niagara Falls. (　　　)
9. It was nice <u>to hear</u> from you. (　　　)
10. I'm going out <u>to meet</u> Jane. (　　　)
11. Mandy went shopping <u>to buy</u> a coat. (　　　)
12. There is something <u>to eat</u> on the table. (　　　)
13. Everybody needs a friend <u>to talk with</u>. (　　　)
14. Did you decide <u>to go</u> to Canada? (　　　)
15. There is nothing <u>to say</u>. (　　　)

**2.** 우리말과 일치하도록 괄호 안의 단어를 알맞게 배열하시오.

1. 저 책은 읽기에 재미있었다. (was/ to/ fun/ that book/ read)

2. 나는 여기에 너를 보러 왔어. (to/ came here/ see/ I/ you)

3. 네가 새로운 직업을 구하다니 운이 좋았구나. (were/ you/ to/ get/ a new job/ lucky)

4. 나는 너를 여기에서 봐서 행복해. (am/ I/ to/ happy/ you/ see/ here)

5. 그녀는 친구들을 만나려고 나갔다. (went out/ she/ see/ to/ her friends)

6. 그런 말을 하다니 너는 어리석었다. (to/ were/ foolish/ say that/ you)

7. 너는 의사선생님 보려고 기다리고 있니? (you/ are/ waiting/ see/ to/ the doctor/ ?)

8. 그 영화는 이해하기 어려웠다. (difficult/ was/ the movie/ understand/ to)

9. 나는 돈을 많이 벌기 위해 두 가지 일을 한다. (working at/ I'm/ two jobs/ make/ a lot of money/ to)

10. 나는 뉴스를 보기위해 TV를 켰다. (the TV/ turned on/ I/ to/ the news/ watch)

# Writing Pattern Practice _「to+동사원형」: 부사

**1.** 목적: …하기 위해서, …하려고

나는 여기에 Henry를 보러 왔어요.  _____

나는 늦지 않으려 했다.  _____

그는 게임에서 이기기 위해 최선을 다했다.  _____

Mandy는 코트를 사기위해 쇼핑 갔다.  _____

Charlie는 일본어를 배우기 위해 도쿄에 갔다.  _____

계좌를 만들려면 제가 무엇이 필요한가요?(open an account)

_____

_____

**2.** 원인: …하니까, …해서

당신을 만나서 반가워요.(It's nice~)  _____

네 소식을 들으니 좋다.(good, hear from you)  _____

나는 그 소식을 들으니 기뻐.(glad)  _____

나는 그 것을 들으니 행복해.(hear that)  _____

**3.** 이유, 판단의 근거: …하다니, …을 보니

그런 행동을 하다니 너는 어리석었다.  _____

그 문제를 해결하다니 너는 천재임에 틀림없다.  _____

아빠가 새로운 직업을 구하시다니 행운이셨다.(get)  _____

**4.** 결과: ~해서 …하다

그는 자라서 훌륭한 가수가 되었다.(grow up to, great)  _____

그녀의 어머니는 80세까지 사셨다.(be)  _____

**5.** 형용사 수식: …하기에

이 책은 읽기에 재미있었다.(fun)  _____

이 강은 수영하기에 매우 위험하다.  _____

저 영화는 이해하기 어려웠다.  _____

# 30 | to부정사의 의미상 주어

Grammar
in
Practice

A: Happy birthday!

B: Thank you. It's so sweet of you to remember my birthday.

A: Why don't you open your present?

B: OK. Wow! It's a sweater. This is just what I wanted.

Grammar
in
Use

**1.** to 부정사도 동사의 한 형태이므로 그 주체가 있다. 이를 '의미상의 주어'라고 한다.

<u>I</u> like **to eat** hamburgers.
문장의 주어 = to부정사의 의미상주어

<u>That hat</u> is too big for <u>you</u> **to wear**.
문장의 주어        to부정사의 의미상주어

**2.** 의미상의 주어로 「for+목적격」을 쓰는 경우가 대부분이다.

These pants are too big **for you** to wear. 이 바지는 네가 입기에 너무 크다.

This tea is too hot **for me** to drink. 이 차는 내가 마시기에 너무 뜨겁다.

It's impossible **for him** to get up early. 그가 일찍 일어나는 것은 불가능하다.

**3.** 의미상의 주어로 「of+목적격」을 쓰는 경우가 있다. <u>사람의 성질, 성품을 나타내는 형용사</u>가 올 때 「It is+형용사+of+의미상주어+to부정사」형태로 쓴다. kind, sweet, stupid, careless, rude 등

It was sweet **of you** to remember my birthday. 내 생일을 기억하다니 너는 다정하구나.

It was careless **of him** to say that. 그런 말을 하다니 그는 부주의했어.

**4.** to부정사의 의미상주어가 문장의 주어나 목적어와 같을 때는 생략한다.

<u>I</u> want **to go out**. 나는 나가고 싶다.
문장의 주어 = to부정사의 의미상주어

I want <u>you</u> **to come** on time. 나는 네가 정각에 오기를 바란다.
문장의 목적어 = to부정사의 의미상주어

**5.** 의미상주어가 일반인이거나 이미 알고 있을 경우 생략한다.

It's good **to be** diligent. 부지런한 것은 좋은 것이다.

It's not a good idea **to skip** that class. 그 수업을 빠지는 것은 좋은 생각이 아니야.

# Unit Test

**1.** 보기와 같이 밑줄 친 to부정사의 의미상 주어에 동그라미 치시오.

> 보기 | It's important for (you) to get there.

1. I want you <u>to get</u> out.
2. It was rude of you <u>to yell</u> at him
3. She decided <u>to leave</u> for Japan.
4. It's important for me <u>to study</u> very hard.
5. It was nice of you <u>to say</u> that.
6. Is it possible for them <u>to get</u> here in five minutes?
7. Do you want me <u>to come</u>?
8. It was careless of you <u>to do</u> that.
9. It was easy for her <u>to answer</u> those questions.
10. This vacuum cleaner is hard for me <u>to use</u>.

**2.** 빈칸에 of 또는 for를 쓰시오.

1. It's kind _____ you to help me.
2. This is easy _____ me to handle.
3. It was stupid _____ him to forget his keys.
4. It's impossible _____ her to speak English fluently.
5. It's sweet _____ you to bring me flowers.
6. It was nice _____ you to e-mail me.
7. Is it difficult _____ them to come here right away?
8. It's time _____ us to go to bed.

**3.** 우리말과 일치하도록 괄호 안의 단어를 알맞게 배열하시오.

1. 저를 도와주시다니 당신 친절하시네요. (kind/ you/ it's/ help me/ of / to)

   _____

2. 그가 농담을 하는 것은 흔치 않다. (it's/ for/ unusual/ make jokes/ him/ to)

   _____

3. 네가 여기에 정각에 오는 것이 가능하니? (it/ on time/ possible/ to/ come here/ is/ for you/ ?)

   _____

4. 그런 말을 하다니 그는 부주의했어. (was/ of / it/ him/ careless/ to/ say that)

   _____

5. 그녀에게는 공부를 열심히 하는 것이 중요하다. (it's / important/ for/ to/ her/ study hard)

   _____

# Writing Pattern Practice

**1.** 「It's ~ for + 목적격 + to 부정사」

이 바지는 네가 입기에 너무 크다.(These pants~) _____

이 차는 내가 마시기에 너무 뜨겁다. _____

그가 일찍 일어나는 것은 불가능하다. _____

그들이 당장 여기에 오는 것은 어렵다.(right away) _____

우리가 잠자리에 들 시간이다. _____

네가 시간을 지키는 것은 중요하다.(be on time) _____

이 청소기는 내가 사용하기 힘들다.(This vacuum cleaner~) _____

그녀가 영어를 유창하게 말하는 것은 불가능하다.(fluently) _____

**2.** 「It's kind, nice, sweet, stupid, careless, rude 등 + of + 목적격 + to 부정사」

내 생일을 기억하다니 너는 다정했어. _____

그런 말을 하다니 그는 부주의했어. _____

나를 도와주다니 너는 친절하다. _____

네가 내게 이메일을 보내서 좋았어. (nice) _____

그녀가 그렇게 하다니 멍청했다.(stupid, do that) _____

그에게 고함지르다니 너는 무례했다.(yell at) _____

**3.** 의미상주어생략: 의미상주어가 문장의 주어나 목적어와 같을 때

나는 가고 싶다.(want) _____

나는 네가 정각에 오기를 원한다. _____

**4.** 의미상주어생략: 의미상주어가 일반인이거나 이미 알고 있을 경우

부지런한 것은 좋은 것이다.(It's~) _____

수업을 빠지는 것은 좋은 생각이 아니야.(skip that class) _____

# 31 | to부정사를 이용한 다양한 표현

**Grammar in Practice**

A: I think I don't speak English very well.

B: No, your English is good enough to have a conversation.

A: Do you really think so?

B: Sure. I do. Don't worry about it.

**Grammar in Use**

**1.** to 부정사를 포함한 어구가 하나의 의미로 문장전체를 꾸며 주는 경우가 있다. 이를 독립부정사 라고 한다.

To make matters worse 설상가상으로

To make matters worse, I fell down on my way here. 설상가상으로 오는 길에 넘어졌어.

To tell the truth 사실을 말하자면

To tell the truth, I don't want to sell my house. 사실, 집을 팔고 싶지는 않아.

Strange to say 이상하게 들리겠지만

Strange to say, but I don't want to make much money.

이상하게 들리겠지만 돈을 많이 벌고 싶지는 않아.

**2.** 정도를 나타내는 to 부정사를 이용한 구문 중 「too+형용사+to부정사」와 「형용사+enough+to부 정사」가 있다.

- 「too+형용사+to부정사」 '~하기에 너무 …하다'

  I'm **too** tired **to** go out. 나는 너무 피곤해서 나갈 수 없다.

  = I can't go out because I'm too tired.

  = I'm so tired that I can't go out.

  It's **too** cold **to** play soccer outside. 너무 추워서 밖에서 축구할 수 없다.

  = We can't play soccer outside because it's too cold.

  = It's so cold that we can't play soccer outside.

- 「형용사+enough+to부정사」 '~하기에 충분히 …하다'

  This bag is big **enough to** carry all of my stuff. 이 가방은 내 짐을 다 넣기에 충분하다.

  = This bag can carry all of my stuff because it is big enough.

  = This bag is so big that I can carry all of my stuff.

  Your English is good **enough to** be understood. 네 영어는 이해하기에 충분히 훌륭해.

  = I can understand your English because it is good enough.

  = Your English is so good that I can understand it.

# Unit Test

**1.** 빈칸에 가장 알맞은 말을 보기에서 골라 써 넣으시오.

> 보기 | to tell the truth    to make matters worse    strange to say

1. I lost my wallet on my way here. _____ , I can't find my keys now.
2. _____ , I think I saw a ghost last night.
3. _____ , your voice sounds terrible.

**2.** to 부정사를 이용한 문장으로 바꾸시오.

1. I'm so tired that I can't go out.
   = I'm _____ tired _____ go out.
2. He's so rich that he can buy a BMW.
   = He's rich _____ _____ buy a BMW.
3. You're so young that you can't drink alcohol.
   = You're _____ young _____ drink alcohol.
4. She's so tall and skinny that she could be a model.
   = She's tall _____ _____ be a model.
5. This book is so difficult that I can't understand.
   = This book is _____ difficult _____ understand.
6. My sister is so smart that she can become a doctor.
   = My sister is smart _____ _____ become a doctor.
7. It's so warm that we can go swimming.
   = It's warm _____ (for us) _____ go swimming.
8. He's so tall that he could become a basketball player.
   = He's tall _____ _____ become a basketball player.

**3.** 우리말과 일치하도록 괄호 안의 단어를 알맞게 배열하시오.

1. 그녀의 영어는 영어 선생님이 되기에 충분하다.
   (is/ good/ her English/ become/ enough/ to/ an English teacher)

   _____

2. 저 코트는 너무 비싸서 살 수 없어요. (too /is / that coat/ expensive/ buy/ to)

   _____

3. 그들은 결혼하기에 충분히 나이 먹었다. (get married/ enough /are/ they/ old/ to)

   _____

4. 나는 너무 놀라서 아무 말도 못했다. (was/ too/ I/ to say/ surprised/ a thing)

   _____

5. 거기까지 걸어가기에는 너무 멀다. (is/ too/ there/ it/ to/ far/ walk)

   _____

# Writing Pattern Practice

**1.** 독립부정사

설상가상으로

_____

설상가상으로, 오는 길에 넘어졌어.(fall down)

_____

사실을 말하자면

_____

사실을 말하자면, 집을 팔고 싶지는 않아.

_____

이상하게 들리겠지만

_____

이상하게 들리겠지만, 돈을 많이 벌고 싶지는 않아.(, but)

_____

**2.** 「too + 형용사 + to부정사」 '~하기에 너무 …하다'

나는 너무 피곤해서 나갈 수 없다.

_____

너무 추워서 밖에서 축구할 수 없다.

_____

Tim은 너무 어려서 운전할 수 없다.

_____

저 코트는 너무 비싸서 살 수 없다.

_____

거기까지 걸어가기에는 너무 멀다.

_____

나는 너무 놀라서 아무 말도 못했다.(say a thing)

_____

그 선반은 닿기에 너무 높다.(reach)

_____

이 가방은 들고 다니기에 너무 무겁다.(carry)

_____

**3.** 「형용사 + enough + to부정사」 '~하기에 충분히 …하다'

너는 저 영화를 볼 충분한 나이다.

_____

네 영어는 이해하기에 충분히 훌륭해.(to be understood)

_____

그들은 결혼하기에 충분히 나이 먹었다.

_____

Sam은 BMW를 살 만큼 충분히 부유하다.

_____

그 소년은 이 책을 이해할 정도로 충분히 똑똑하다.(smart)

_____

그녀는 모델이 되기에 충분히 키가 크다.

_____

Unit

# 32 | 동명사의 역할

Grammar in Practice

A: Why were you late to your first class?

B: I *slept in.

A: I thought so.

B: Getting up early every day is very difficult for me.

*sleep in 늦잠자다

---

Grammar in Use

**1.** 동명사는 「동사원형+ing」형태로 명사 기능을 가지며 문장 안에서 주어, 목적어, 보어, 전치사의 목적어 역할을 한다.

eat (먹다) → **eating** (먹는 것)

cry (울다) → **crying** (우는 것)

**2.** 동명사는 주어역할을 한다. 가주어 it을 쓰는 경우도 가끔 있다.

**Exercising** every day is good for your health. 매일 운동하는 것은 건강에 좋다.

**Being** kind to everyone is not easy. 모두에게 친절하기란 쉽지 않다.

It was nice **talking** to you. 너와 이야기 한 것은 좋았어.

**3.** 동명사는 목적어역할을 한다.

I like **playing** soccer. 나는 축구하는 것을 좋아한다.

I hate **eating** alone. 나는 혼자 먹는 것을 싫어해.

The car needs **repairing**. 그 차는 수리를 필요로 한다.

| MORE TIPS | 모든 동사가 동명사를 목적어로 가질 수 있는 것은 아니다. UNIT 49 참조

**4.** 동명사는 보어역할을 한다.

My hobby is **watching** movies. 나의 취미는 영화를 보는 것이다.

His goal is **buying** a BMW. 그의 목표는 BMW를 사는 것이다.

My part time job is **cooking** in a restaurant. 내 부업은 식당에서 요리하는 것이다.

**5.** 동명사는 전치사의 목적어역할을 한다.

Thank you for **helping** me. 나를 도와줘서 고마워.

I feel like **dancing**. 나는 춤추고 싶은 기분이다.

I'm used to **sleeping** on the bus. 나는 버스에서 자는 데 익숙하다.

| MORE TIPS | 전치사가 to일 경우 to부정사의 to와 잘 구분해야 한다.

# Unit Test

**1.** 밑줄 친 「동사+ing」가 현재분사로 쓰였으면 '현', 동명사로 쓰였으면 '동'이라고 쓰시오.

1. I'm <u>vacuuming</u> the floor. (　　)
2. I enjoyed <u>having</u> dinner with you. (　　)
3. Look at the man <u>smiling</u> over there. (　　)
4. He hates <u>eating</u> alone. (　　)
5. <u>Being</u> kind to everyone is difficult. (　　)
6. She's <u>talking</u> on the phone. (　　)
7. Do you like <u>visiting</u> other countries? (　　)
8. My sister is <u>learning</u> to drive. (　　)
9. He isn't <u>working</u> today. (　　)
10. It was <u>raining</u>, so we couldn't play tennis. (　　)

**2.** 밑줄 친 동명사가 주어역할을 하면 '주' 목적어역할을 하면 '목' 보어역할을 하면 '보' 전치사의 목적어 역할을 하면 '전'이라고 쓰시오.

1. <u>Getting up</u> early isn't easy. (　　)
2. <u>Jogging</u> is good for you. (　　)
3. He quit <u>smoking</u>. (　　)
4. <u>Catching</u> a taxi isn't easy in New York. (　　)
5. I'm interested in <u>reading</u> that book. (　　)
6. Do you like <u>eating</u> out? (　　)
7. Are you used to <u>exercising</u> every day? (　　)

**3.** 우리말과 일치하도록 괄호 안의 단어를 알맞게 배열하시오.

1. 나는 너를 돕는 것을 꺼리지 않아. (I/ mind/ helping/ don't/ you)

2. 비가 오기 시작했다. (started/ it/ raining)

3. 나는 다른 나라 방문하는 것을 즐긴다. (enjoy/ visiting/ I/ other countries)

4. 그녀는 차로 여행하는 것을 더 좋아한다. (prefers/ she/ by car/ traveling)

5. 덜 먹는 것이 네 건강에 좋다. (is/ good/ for your health/ eating less)

6. 눈이 그쳤다. (stopped/ it/ snowing)

7. 그들은 계속 걸었다. (kept/ they/ walking)

# Writing Pattern Practice _동명사「동사~ing」

**1.**   **주어역할**

매일 운동하는 것은 건강에 좋다.

모두에게 친절하기란 쉽지 않다.(be kind)

매일 일찍 일어나는 것은 어렵다.

너와 이야기 한 것은 좋았어.(It was nice~)

거기에 한시간만에 도착한 것은 불가능해요.(Getting there~)


**2.**   **목적어역할**

나는 축구 하는 것을 좋아한다.

나는 혼자 먹는 것을 싫어해.(hate)

그 차는 수리를 필요로 한다.(repairing)

나는 모든 종류의 영화 보는 것을 즐긴다.(all kinds of movies)


그는 담배를 끊었다.(quit)

덜 먹는 것이 네 건강에 좋다.(Eating less~)

눈이 오기 시작했다.(start)

눈이 그쳤다.


**3.**   **보어역할**

나의 취미는 영화를 보는 것이다.(watch movies)


나의 부업은 식당에서 요리하는 것이다.(My part time job is~)


나의 좋아하는 스포츠는 테니스 치는 것이다.(favorite)


**4.**   **전치사의 목적어역할**

나를 도와줘서 고마워.(Thank you for~)

나는 춤추고 싶은 기분이다.(feel like)

나는 버스에서 자는 데 익숙하다.(be used to)

나는 너를 돕는 것을 꺼리지 않는다.

나는 너를 보는 것을 손꼽아 기다리고 있다.(look forward to)

**Unit**

# 33 | 목적어로 쓰이는 부정사와 동명사

Grammar
in
Practice

A: What's wrong?
B: I don't know. My daughter won't stop crying.
A: I think she is hungry.
B: Oh, I forgot to feed her.

Grammar
in
Use

1. to 부정사만 목적어 취하는 동사는 want, need, hope, expect(예상하다), decide(결정하다), plan, would like, would love 등이다.
   **What a surprise! I didn't expect to see you here.** 놀래라! 너를 여기서 볼 줄 몰랐어.

2. 동명사만 목적어 취하는 동사는 finish, mind, avoid(피하다), stop, enjoy, give up(포기하다), consider 등이다.
   **I finished working.** 나는 일을 마쳤다.

3. to 부정사와 동명사 모두 목적어로 취하는 동사는 like, love, prefer, hate, start, begin, continue 등이다. 둘 사이의 의미 차이는 거의 없다.
   **It began to rain. = It began raining.** 비가 오기 시작했다.

4. 동명사와 to 부정사 모두 목적어로 취하면서 서로 뜻이 달라지는 동사는 remember, forget, try 등이다.
   • remember+동명사: ~한 것을 기억하다
   • remember+to부정사: ~할 것을 기억하다
   **Remember to go to see a doctor today.** 오늘 병원 가는 거 기억해라.
   **I remember seeing him once before.** 지난번 그를 만난 거 기억한다.

   • forget+동명사: ~한 것을 잊다(forget about ~ing의 형태로 주로 쓰인다)
   • forget+to부정사: ~할 것을 잊다
   **I forgot about calling you.** 너에게 전화한 걸 잊었어.
   **I forgot to call you.** 너에게 전화할 것을 잊었어.

   • try+동명사: 시험 삼아 ~해보다
   • try+to부정사: ~하기 위해 노력하다
   **I tried eating Mexican food.** 나는 멕시코 음식을 먹어보았다.
   **I tried to help him.** 나는 그를 도우려 했다.

   **| MORE TIPS |** stop ~ing와 stop to + V
   stop 또한 「stop+동명사」, 「stop+to부정사」의 형태로 쓰이는데, stop+동명사는 '…하는 것을 멈추다,' stop+to 부정사는 '…하기 위해 멈추다' 라는 뜻이다. 다만 「stop+to부정사」에서 to부정사는 stop의 목적어가 아니라 '…하기 위해서' 라는 부사적용법이라는 점이 특이하다.

# Unit Test

**1.** 그림의 상황에 맞는 말을 보기와 같이 동명사나 to부정사의 형태로 쓰시오.

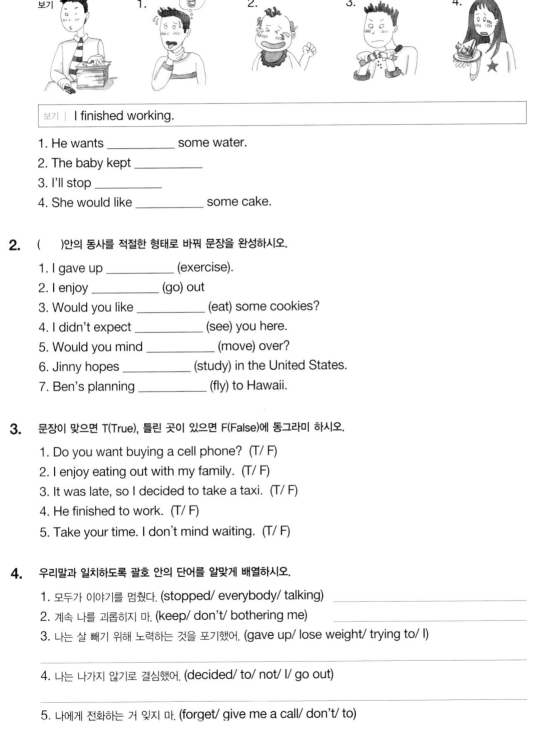

| 보기 | I finished working. |
|------|---------------------|

1. He wants _____ some water.
2. The baby kept _____
3. I'll stop _____
4. She would like _____ some cake.

**2.** (   )안의 동사를 적절한 형태로 바꿔 문장을 완성하시오.

1. I gave up _____ (exercise).
2. I enjoy _____ (go) out
3. Would you like _____ (eat) some cookies?
4. I didn't expect _____ (see) you here.
5. Would you mind _____ (move) over?
6. Jinny hopes _____ (study) in the United States.
7. Ben's planning _____ (fly) to Hawaii.

**3.** 문장이 맞으면 T(True), 틀린 곳이 있으면 F(False)에 동그라미 하시오.

1. Do you want buying a cell phone?  (T/ F)
2. I enjoy eating out with my family.  (T/ F)
3. It was late, so I decided to take a taxi.  (T/ F)
4. He finished to work.  (T/ F)
5. Take your time. I don't mind waiting.  (T/ F)

**4.** 우리말과 일치하도록 괄호 안의 단어를 알맞게 배열하시오.

1. 모두가 이야기를 멈췄다. (stopped/ everybody/ talking) _____
2. 계속 나를 괴롭히지 마. (keep/ don't/ bothering me) _____
3. 나는 살 빼기 위해 노력하는 것을 포기했어. (gave up/ lose weight/ trying to/ I)

_____

4. 나는 나가지 않기로 결심했어. (decided/ to/ not/ I/ go out)

_____

5. 나에게 전화하는 거 잊지 마. (forget/ give me a call/ don't/ to)

_____

# Writing Pattern Practice

**1.** 「I want, need, hope, expect, decide, plan, would like, would love + to 부정사」

나는 피자를 먹기를 원한다. _____

나는 일본으로 떠나지 않기로 결심했다.(leave for) _____

나는 너를 여기서 볼 줄 몰랐어.(expect) _____


**2.** 「I finish, mind, avoid, stop, enjoy, give up, consider + 동명사」

나는 일을 마쳤다.(finish) _____

나는 너를 돕는 것을 꺼리지 않는다. _____

나는 영어배우는 것을 즐긴다. _____


**3.** 「I like, love, prefer, hate, start, begin, continue + to 부정사/ 동명사」

나는 영화 보는 것을 좋아한다.(watch movies) _____

나는 요리하는 것을 좋아한다.(love) _____

나는 집에서 축구경기를 보는 것을 더 좋아한다. _____

나는 혼자 있는 것을 싫어한다. _____

눈이 오기 시작했다.(start) _____

비가 오기 시작했다.(begin) _____

나는 계속 이야기했다. _____


**4.** 「remember, forget, try + to 부정사/ 동명사」

오늘 병원 가는 거 기억해라.(go to see a doctor) _____

나는 지난번 그를 만난 거 기억한다.(~once before) _____

나에게 전화하는 거 잊지 마.(give me a call) _____

나는 너에게 전화한 걸 잊었어. _____

나는 너에게 전화할 것을 잊었어. _____

나는 멕시코 음식을 먹어 봤다. _____

나는 그를 돕기 위해 노력했다. _____

# REVIEW 1

**1.** 다음 우리말을 영어문장으로 바꿔 쓰시오.

① 나는 나가기를 원한다. → _____
② 피아노 치는 것은 나의 취미다.(동명사이용) → _____
③ 나는 자는 것을 즐긴다. → _____
④ Jane은 코트를 살 필요가 있다. → _____
⑤ 나는 아침에 샤워하는 것에 익숙하다. → _____

**2.** 다음 영어 문장을 우리말로 쓰시오.

① My goal is to become a singer → _____
② You were foolish to do such a thing. → _____
③ This book was fun to read. → _____
④ I remember seeing him once before. → _____
⑤ I forgot to call you. → _____

**3.** 다음 중 틀린 곳을 바르게 고치시오.

① I hope seeing you soon. → _____
② Ted wants go to the party. → _____
③ You seem to are in good health. → _____
④ Dennis needs a book read. → _____
⑤ I need someone to talk. → _____
⑥ It's too cold going out. → _____
⑦ You're enough old to go to school. → _____
⑧ I didn't expect seeing you here. → _____
⑨ Do you mind to open the window? → _____
⑩ Jane finished to work. → _____

**4.** 둘 중에서 알맞은 것을 골라 동그라미 하시오.

① I want (to see/ seeing) you again.
② You need (to exercise/ exercising).
③ Did you finish (to work/ working)?
④ Jason finally gave up (to gamble/ gambling).
⑤ Caroline hopes (to study/ studying) abroad.
⑥ I enjoy (to eat/ eating)
⑦ Have you considered (to change/ changing) your job?
⑧ Olivia decided not (to leave/ leaving).
⑨ Are you planning (to go/ going) to Hawaii?
⑩ I couldn't avoid (to wear/ wearing) the same clothes again.

# REVIEW 2

**1.** 밑줄 친 to 부정사와 문장 안에서 같은 역할을 하는 것은?

> 보기 | I came here <u>to see</u> you.

① What do I need <u>to open</u> an account?
② I need something <u>to eat</u>.
③ It's important <u>to exercise</u> every day.
④ I told you <u>to come</u> on time.
⑤ Everybody needs someone <u>to talk to</u>.

**2.** 밑줄 친 동명사와 문장 안에서 같은 역할을 하는 것은?

> 보기 | I like <u>playing</u> soccer.

① <u>Being</u> kind to everyone is not easy.
② Thank you for <u>helping</u> me.
③ That car needs <u>repairing</u>.
④ It was nice <u>talking</u> to you.
⑤ I'm used to <u>getting up</u> early.

**3.** 어법상 맞는 문장을 고르시오.

① I feel like throw up.
② I'm used to sleep in.
③ Thank you for helping me.
④ It was nice talk to you.
⑤ His goal is be a doctor.

**4.** 빈칸에 들어갈 수 <u>없는</u> 말은?

> It was _____ of you to say that.

① kind          ② careless
③ rude          ④ stupid
⑤ necessary

[5~6] 빈칸에 들어갈 알맞은 말은?

**5.** _____ makes people happy.

① I smile brightly
② Smiling brightly
③ For smiling brightly
④ Smile brightly
⑤ Smile brightly and

**6.** It's _____ cold to play soccer outside.
= We can't play soccer outside because it's too cold.

① so
② as
③ very
④ too
⑤ enough

**7.** 밑줄 친 것의 역할이 <u>다른</u> 하나를 고르시오.

① I need something <u>to write with</u>.
② Give me something <u>to drink</u>.
③ Do you need a chair <u>to sit on</u>?
④ I don't have time <u>to meet my friends</u>.
⑤ It was sweet of you <u>to do that</u>.

**8.** 밑줄 친 것이 부사 역할을 하는 것을 고르시오.

① We want <u>to take a coffee break</u>.
② It's dangerous <u>to drive fast</u>.
③ I forgot <u>to call Mary</u>.
④ What do I have to do <u>to lose weight</u>?
⑤ Jennifer needs someone <u>to rely on</u>.

**9.** 다음 글을 읽고 빈칸에 공통으로 들어갈 알맞은 말을 고르시오.

① to          ② as
③ at          ④ too
⑤ enough

People like board games a lot because they are fun _____ play. Some games are short, and others can take all day.

We can play with two or sometimes up to eight people. There are many kinds of board games. We can draw cards or roll dice _____ move our piece around. Win or lose, it's a lot of fun. One of the most popular board games in the U.S. is 'monopoly.' It's similar to 'Blue Marble' in Korea.

\* similar 비슷한

# *Chapter 7 | 분사

현재분사 | Unit 34
과거분사 | Unit 35
분사구문 | Unit 36

# 34 | 현재분사

**Grammar in Practice**

A: Look at the baby sitting in the stroller.
B: How cute!
A: He's smiling at us.
B: Yes, he is. He has a beautiful smile.

---

**Grammar in Use**

**1.** 현재분사의 형태는 「동사+ ~ing」이다.

| | |
|---|---|
| • cry 울다 | – crying 울고 있는 |
| • sing 노래하다 | – singing 노래하고 있는 |
| • study 공부하다 | – studying 공부하고 있는 |
| • tire 피곤하게 하다 | – tiring 피곤하게 하(고 있)는 |
| • bore 지루하게 하다 | – boring 지루하게 하(고 있)는 |
| • depress 우울하게 하다 | – depressing 우울하게 하(고 있)는 |
| • embarrass 당황하게 하다 | – embarrassing 당황하게 하(고 있)는 |

**2.** 현재 분사는 문장 안에서 형용사역할을 한다.

● 명사를 꾸며준다.
Look at the **smiling** baby. He's so cute. 저 웃고 있는 아기를 봐요. 정말 귀여워요.
I saw a **boring** movie last night. 나는 어젯밤 지루한 영화를 봤다.
My sister is an **interesting** person. 언니는 재미있는 사람이다.

● 목적어나 부사구 등과 함께 명사를 꾸밀 경우 명사 뒤로 간다.
The girl **playing** the piano is my daughter. 피아노를 치고 있는 소녀가 내 딸이다.
Do you know the man **sitting** on the bench? 너는 벤치에 앉아 있는 남자를 아니?

● 주어의 상황을 설명하는 주격보어 역할을 한다.
My father is **washing** his car. 아버지는 세차를 하고 계신다.
My mother is **doing** the laundry. 어머니는 빨래를 하고 계신다.
My brother is **watching** a movie. 오빠는 영화를 보고 있다.
I'm **feeding** the dog. 나는 개밥을 주고 있다.
This movie seems **interesting**. 이 영화는 재미있는 것 같다.

● 목적어의 상황을 설명하는 목적격보어 역할을 한다.
I saw John **cheating** on a test. 나는 John이 커닝 하는 것을 봤다.
I heard a baby **crying** last night. 나는 어젯밤 아기 우는 소리를 들었다.
I'm sorry I kept you **waiting**. 미안해요. 당신을 계속 기다리게 했어요.

# Unit Test

**1.** 그림에 맞게 알맞는 현재분사를 빈칸에 넣으시오.

1.    2.    3.

1. The baby is _____
2. He saw her _____
3. We're _____ a soccer game on TV.


**2.** 밑줄 친 현재분사가 꾸미는 명사에 동그라미 하시오.

1. I saw a <u>crying</u> child in the park.
2. Do you know the woman <u>talking</u> to James?
3. Look at the <u>smiling</u> baby.
4. It was a <u>boring</u> concert.
5. The man <u>standing</u> over there is my boyfriend.


**3.** 밑줄 친 현재분사를 주격보어와 목적격보어로 구분하시오.

1. That movie seems <u>exciting</u>. (        )
2. I smell something <u>burning</u>. (        )
3. I saw you <u>walking</u> with Kate. (        )
4. Did you see me <u>cheating</u>? (        )
5. Is Mary <u>boring</u>? (        )


**4.** 우리말과 일치하도록 괄호 안의 단어를 알맞게 배열하시오.

1. 내 일은 피곤하게 한다. (is/ tiring/ my work)

2. 벤치 위에 앉아 있는 그 남자는 Ted입니다. (Ted/ is/ sitting/ on/ the man/ the bench)

3. 무대에서 춤추는 그 여자를 알아요? (Do you know/ dancing/ the woman/ on/ the stage/ ?)

# Writing Pattern Practice

**1.** 「현재분사 + 명사」

그 웃고 있는 아기

그 웃고 있는 아기를 봐요.

지루한 영화

나는 어젯밤 지루한 영화를 봤다.

재미있는 사람(an interesting~)

언니는 재미있는 사람이다.

지루한 콘서트

그것은 지루한 콘서트였어.

**2.** 「명사 + 현재분사 + 목적어/부사구」

저쪽에서 웃고 있는 남자(over there)

저쪽에서 웃고 있는 남자를 봐.

피아노를 치고 있는 소녀

피아노를 치고 있는 소녀가 내 딸이다.

벤치에 앉아 있는 남자

너는 벤치에 앉아 있는 남자를 아니?

저쪽에 서 있는 남자

저쪽에 서 있는 남자가 내 남자친구야.

**3.** 「주어 + 동사 + 현재분사(주격보어)」

나는 샤워를 하고 있다.(take)

나는 개 밥 주고 있다.(feed the dog)

너 공부 열심히 하고 있구나.

아버지는 세차를 하고 계시다.

우리는 파티를 하고 있다.(have)

그 영화는 흥미로운 것 같다.(seem)

**4.** 「주어 + 동사 + 목적어 + 현재분사(목적격보어)」

나는 네가 Kate와 걷는 것을 봤어.

나는 John이 커닝 하는 것을 봤다.

나는 어젯밤 아기가 우는 것을 들었다.

너는 그들이 싸우는 것 들었니?

I'm sorry. 당신을 계속 기다리게 했어요.(keep)

# 35 | 과거분사

A: How have you been?
B: I've been busy working.
A: How's your new job?
B: Good. I'm really satisfied with it.

**1.** 과거분사의 형태는 「동사원형+ ed 또는 불규칙변화」이다.

- use 사용하다     – used 사용되어진
- make 만들다     – made 만들어진
- love 사랑하다    – loved 사랑받는
- steal 훔치다     – stolen 훔쳐진(도난당한)
- interest 관심을 끌다  – interested 관심이 있는
- bore 지루하게 하다  – bored 지루함을 느끼는
- satisfy 만족시키다  – satisfied 만족함을 느끼는

**2.** 과거분사는 문장 안에서 주로 형용사역할을 한다.

- 명사를 꾸며준다.
  Eric bought a **used** car. Eric은 중고차를 샀다.
  There are some **fallen** leaves on the ground. 바닥에 낙엽이 좀 있다.

- 목적어나 부사구 등과 함께 명사를 꾸밀 경우 명사 뒤로 간다.
  English is one of the languages **spoken** in many countries. 영어는 많은 나라에서 말해지는 언어 중의 하나이다.
  Hotels have rooms **filled** with sheets and towels. 호텔방엔 시트와 수건이 가득하다.

- 주어의 상황을 설명하는 주격보어역할을 한다.
  You look **tired** today. 너 오늘 피곤해 보인다.
  He seems **interested** in classical music. 그는 클래식 음악에 관심이 있는 듯하다.

- 목적어의 상황을 설명하는 목적격 보어 역할을 한다.
  I found the street **crowded** with children. 거리에는 어린 아이들로 혼잡했다.
  I want this homework **finished tonight**. 오늘 밤에 이 숙제를 끝내고 싶어.

**3.** 현재완료나 수동태를 만들 때 쓰기도 한다.
  I have **known** Kate for 5 years. 나는 Kate를 5년 동안 알아왔다.
  "How have you **been**?" "I've **been** busy." 그동안 어떻게 지냈어? 그동안 바빴어.
  This bag was **made** in Italy. 이 가방은 이탈리아제다.
  "Were you **invited** to the party?" "Yes, I was." 너 파티에 초대 받았어? 응, 받았어.

# Unit Test

**1.** 보기의 동사를 적절하게 바꿔 빈칸에 넣으시오.

| 보기 | interest | break | fall |

1. The window is _____
2. There are some _____ leaves on the ground.
3. I'm _____ in movies.

**2.** 밑줄 친 과거분사가 꾸미는 명사에 동그라미 하시오.

1. I saw some <u>fallen</u> leaves in the park.
2. Look at the cars <u>parked</u> on the street.
3. This is the university <u>attended</u> by Britney Spears.
4. This is a song <u>sung</u> by Beatles.
5. I bought a book <u>written</u> by O'Henry.

**3.** 밑줄 친 과거분사를 주격보어와 목적격보어로 구분해 쓰시오.

1. I'm <u>tired</u>. (          )
2. Mark seemed <u>interested</u> in music. (          )
3. I found the store <u>closed</u>. (          )
4. Are you <u>satisfied</u> with your job? (          )
5. Do you want your hair <u>permed</u>? (          )

**4.** 우리말과 일치하도록 괄호 안의 단어를 알맞게 배열하시오.

1. 저 주차된 차를 봐. (the/ look at/ car/ parked)

_____

2. 그는 그의 새로운 일에 만족스러워 보였다. (looked/ his new job/ satisfied/ he/ with)

_____

3. 호텔방에는 시트와 수건이 가득하다. (have rooms/ sheets and towels/ hotels/ filled with)

_____

# Writing Pattern Practice

**1.** 「과거분사 + 명사」

중고차(use)

Eric은 중고차를 샀다.

낙엽

바닥에 낙엽이 좀 있다.(on the ground)

그 부서진 문

그 부서진 문을 봐.(look)


**2.** 「명사 + 과거분사 + 목적어/부사구」

거리에 주차된 차들

거리에 주차된 차들을 봐.

많은 나라에서 말해지는 언어중 하나(one of the languages)

영어는 많은 나라에서 말해지는 언어중 하나이다.

Britney Spears가 다니던 대학교(attend)

이것이 Britney Spears가 다니던 대학교이다.

O'Henry가 쓴 책(O'Henry에 의해 씌어진 책)

나는 O'Henry가 쓴 책을 샀다.


**3.** 「주어 + 동사 + 과거분사(주격보어)」

나는 피곤하다.(tire:피곤하게하다)

나는 지루하다.(bore:지루하게하다)

나는 당황스럽다.(embarrass:당황하게하다)

나는 신난다.(excite:신나게하다)

나는 관심 있다.(interest:관심을 끌다)

나는 혼란스럽다.(confuse:혼란스럽게 하다)

나는 실망했다.(disappoint:실망시키다)

나는 놀랐다.(surprise:놀라게 하다)

나는 충격 받았다.(shock:충격을 주다)

나는 만족한다.(satisfy:만족시키다)

나는 우울하다.(depress:우울하게하다)


**4.** 「주어 + 동사 + 목적어 + 과거분사(목적격보어)」

나는 가게가 문닫은 것을 알았다.(find)

나는 내 신발이 수선되길 원해요.(repair)

나는 내 이름이 불리는 것을 들었다.(call)

## Unit 36 분사구문

**Grammar in Practice**

A: Where did you go last night?

    I called you many times.

B: I was sleeping.

    Feeling tired, I went to bed very early.

---

**Grammar in Use**

**1.** 분사구문이란 분사를 이용하여 '부사절'을 '부사구'로 간단히 표현하는 것을 말한다.

<u>When I walked down the street</u>, I met Kelly. 라는 문장이 있다고 가정하자. 이때 부사절의
    부사절       주절

접속사(when)를 생략하고, 부사절의 주어가 주절의 주어(I)와 같은 경우, 주어도 생략할 수 있다.
그리고 부사절의 동사를 분사형태(walking)로 바꾸면 분사구문이 완성된다.
그러므로 앞의 긴 문장을 <u>Walking down the street</u>, I met Kelly. 형태로 짧게 말할 수 있다.
                                   부사구

| 분사구문 만들기 정리 | |
|---|---|
| ① 부사절의 접속사를 생략한다.<br>② 부사절의 주어가 주절의 주어와 같으면 생략한다.<br>③ 부사절의 동사를 「동사원형-ing」형태로 바꾼다. | ① ~~After~~ I had lunch, I went out for a walk.<br>② ~~I~~ had lunch, I went out for a walk.<br>③ Having lunch, I went out for a walk. |

**2.** 다양한 형태의 분사구문

- 분사구문이 Being으로 시작할 경우, Being을 생략할 수 있다.

  (Being) Tired, I went to bed very early. 피곤해서, 일찍 잠자리에 들었다.

- '분사구문의 부정'은 분사구문 앞에 not, never 등의 부정어를 쓴다.

  <u>Not having</u> much money, I can't buy that house. 돈이 많지 않아서, 나는 그 집을 살 수 없다.

**3.** 다양한 의미의 분사구문

- When I saw him at the mall, I felt happy.

  → **Seeing him at the mall**, I felt happy. (시간) 그를 mall에서 봤을 때, 나는 행복했다.

- Because I was so busy, I couldn't call you.

  → **Being so busy**, I couldn't call you. (이유) 너무 바빠서, 나는 네게 전화할 수 없었다.

- If you go straight, you'll see the hospital.

  → **Going straight**, you'll see the hospital. (조건) 곧장 가면, 병원이 보일 거야.

- While she was talking on the phone, she washed the dishes.

  → **Talking on the phone**, she washed the dishes. (동시동작) 전화통화를 하면서, 그녀는 설거지를 했다.

**| MORE TIPS | 숙어처럼 쓰이는 분사구문**

분사구문의 주어가 일반인(we, you, they)인 경우, 생략하고 숙어처럼 쓰는 경우가 많다.
- generally/ frankly/strictly speaking: 일반적으로/솔직히/엄밀히 말해서
- judging from: ~로 판단하건대 • considering that: ~를 감안하건대

  **Generally speaking**, Americans love coffee. 일반적으로 말해서, 미국인들은 커피를 좋아한다.

# Unit Test

**1.** 둘 중 알맞은 것을 고르시오.

1. (Shocking/ Shocked) at the news, I couldn't say anything.

2. (Turning/ Turned) right, go straight for two blocks.

3. (Not having/ Having not) a cell phone, I couldn't call you.

4. (Tiring/ Tired) after work, I took a rest.

5. Are you going to stand there (doing/ done) nothing?

6. (Working/ Worked) all day, I was exhausted.    *exhausted 기진맥진한

7. (Watching/ Watched) a video, he fell asleep.

8. (Putting on/ Put on) his coat, he went out.

9. (Not knowing/ Not known) what to say, she kept quiet.

10. (Writing/ Written) in French, I can't read that book.

**2.** 보기와 같이 문장의 밑줄친 부분을 분사구문으로 바꾸어 쓰시오.

> 보기 |  When I saw her, I was surprised.
> → Seeing her, I was surprised.

1. After I talked to you, I felt better.

→ _____ , I felt better.

2. Because I had no time, I couldn't see her.

→ _____ , I couldn't see her.

3. If you go straight, you'll see a tall building.

→ _____ , you'll see a tall building.

4. As he waved his hand, he went out.

→ _____ , he went out.

**3.** 우리말과 일치하도록 괄호안의 동사를 이용하여 빈칸에 알맞은 말을 써 넣으시오.

1. 노래를 부르며, 나는 집안 청소를 했다.

_____ (Sing) a song, I cleaned my house.

2. 시간이 충분하지 않았기 때문에, 나는 뛰어서 학교에 갔다.

_____ (Not, have) enough time, I ran home.

3. 흥분에서, 나는 위아래로 뛰었다.

_____ (Excite), I jumped up and down.

# Writing Pattern Practice

**1.** 시간과 이유를 나타내는 분사구문

나를 봤을 때, 그는 도망갔다.(run away) _____

그 소식을 들었을 때, 나는 놀랐었다.(hear, be surprised) _____

내 방에 들어가서, 나는 TV를 켰다. (go into, turn on) _____

시간이 없었기 때문에, 나는 서둘렀다.(no time, hurry up) _____


**2.** 조건과 부대상황을 나타내는 분사구문

우회전하면, 당신은 은행을 보게 될 거에요. (turn, a bank) _____

음악을 들으면서, 너는 공부하면 안 된다. (listen to music, should not) _____

껌을 씹으면서, 그는 계속 말했다.(chew gum, keep talking) _____


**3.** 부정 분사구문

점심을 안 먹어서, 나는 배가 고팠었다.(have) _____

차가 없어서, 그녀는 여기에 걸어왔다.(walk here) _____


**4.** Being이 생략된 분사구문

직장에서 피곤해서, 나는 집에 일찍 왔다.(at work, come home) _____

프랑스어로 쓰여져서 나는 그 책을 읽을 수 없다.(in French, that book) _____

**1.** 다음 우리말을 영어로 바꿔 쓰시오.

① 피아노치고 있는 소녀       → the _____

② 거리에 주차된 차들       → the _____

③ 운동장에서 축구하는 남자(in the field)       → the _____

④ 벤치에 앉아있는 남자       → the _____

⑤ 저쪽에 서있는 여자       → the _____


**2.** 다음 영어 문장을 우리말로 쓰시오.

① I saw him dancing.       → _____

② I heard a baby crying.       → _____

③ I kept you waiting.       → _____

④ I found the bookshelves filled with novels.       → _____

⑤ Smiling brightly, he walked to me.       → _____


**3.** 다음 중 틀린 곳을 바르게 고치시오.

① I saw John walked down the street.       → _____

② My brother is watch a movie now.       → _____

③ The story is so excited.       → _____

④ Is Terry take a shower now?       → _____

⑤ The movie was bored.       → _____

⑥ He seems interesting in music       → _____

⑦ I'm pleasing to meet you.       → _____

⑧ Eaten too much, I couldn't eat another bite.       → _____

⑨ Knowing not her, I didn't say hello.       → _____

⑩ Finished her homework, she went to bed.       → _____


**4.** 둘 중에서 알맞은 것을 골라 동그라미 하시오.

① The movie was so (shocking/ shocked).

② The concert was (boring/ bored)

③ I feel (embarrassing/ embarrassed).

④ The soccer game was (exciting/ excited).

⑤ It's raining again? The weather is so (depressing/ depressed).

⑥ Are you (interesting/ interested) in jazz?

⑦ You cheated again. I'm so (disappointing/ disappointed)

⑧ (Being mean/ Be mean) to others, he has few friends.

⑨ (Not feeling/ Feeling not) well, I came back home early.

⑩ (Listening/ Listened) to music, he studied math.

# REVIEW 2

**1.** 밑줄 친 현재분사 중 문장 안에서 보어역할을 하는 것을 고르시오.

① Look at the <u>crying</u> baby.
② The man <u>standing</u> over there is my brother.
③ I saw a <u>boring</u> movie.
④ Do you know the man <u>playing</u> soccer?
⑤ I heard someone <u>crying</u>.

**2.** 밑줄 친 과거분사 중 문장 안에서의 역할이 <u>다른</u> 하나를 고르시오.

① Eric bought a <u>used</u> car.
② There're some <u>fallen</u> leaves on the ground.
③ This is a song <u>written</u> by Beatles.
④ Hotels have rooms <u>filled</u> with sheets and towels.
⑤ I have <u>known</u> her for a long time.

**3.** 어법상 맞는 문장을 고르시오.

① The news was surprising.
② The book is so bored.
③ Eaten something, he walked into the room.
④ My sister is interested person.
⑤ Knowing not what to do, I just sat on the chair.

**4.** 다음 빈칸에 차례로 들어갈 말은?

> My car is _____ all over. I want it_____.

① dent - repair
② denting - repairing
③ dented - repaired
④ denting - repaired
⑤ dented - repairing

**5.** 밑줄 친 부분이 <u>다르게</u> 쓰인 하나를 고르시오.

① I <u>made</u> some spaghetti for my sister.
② This bag was <u>made</u> in Italy.
③ You look <u>tired</u> today.
④ I met a girl <u>named</u> Emily
⑤ Have you heard of a game <u>called</u> Warcraft?

**6.** 다음 밑줄 친 부분과 바꿔 쓸 수 있는 것을 고르시오.

> <u>Living</u> far away, she seldom comes for Christmas.

① Though she lives
② Before she lives
③ When she lives
④ As she lives
⑤ Even if she lives

**7.** 다음 글을 읽고 빈칸에 들어갈 말로 알맞게 짝지어진 것을 고르시오.

① surprise-interest
② surprising-interesting
③ surprised-interested
④ surprising-interested
⑤ surprised-interesting

Do you know what the heaviest animal on land is? It's the elephant.

How about the heaviest coastal animal? It's the elephant seal.

Male seals can weigh up to 4,000 kilograms. That's twice the weight of a car. Isn't it _____? You must be _____ in what they eat.

Strangely they don't eat very big foods. They eat octopus, squid, and mussels. They often eat many of them for one meal.

\*elephant seal 바다표범 \*squid 오징어
\*mussel 홍합

※ **Chapter 8** | **수동태**

능동태와 수동태 | Unit 37
수동태표현 | Unit 38

# Unit
# 37 | 능동태와 수동태

A: What is it?
B: I don't know. It's written in Japanese.
A: Let me see. You're invited to Akiko's birthday party.
B: Really? That's great.

1. 행위를 누구의 관점에서 표현하느냐에 따라 능동태와 수동태로 나눌 수 있다.

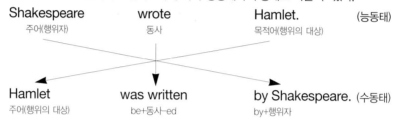

2. 능동태는 '누가~한다'로 행위를 하는 행위자에 초점을 두는 반면 수동태는 '누가~받는다/ 당한다'로 행위를 당하는 대상에 초점을 둔다.
   (능동태) A mosquito bit me. 모기가 나를 물었다.
   (수동태) I **was bitten** by a mosquito. 나는 모기에게 물렸다.

3. 수동태는 행위자가 중요하지 않을 때나 행위자가 누구인지 짐작할 수 있을 때 또는 행위의 대상을 강조할 때 사용한다.
   Rome **wasn't built** in a day. 로마는 하루아침에 이루어지지 않았다.
   English **is spoken** in many countries. 많은 나라에서 영어가 말해진다.

4. 수동태에서 by+행위자는 일반 사람이나 중요하지 않을 경우 생략될 수 있다.
   He **is called** Mr. Perfect. 그는 완벽주의자라고 불려진다.
   The window **is broken**. 창문이 깨져있다.

5. 수동태의 시제에 따른 변화는 다음과 같다.
   (현재) Jane **is loved** by everybody. Jane은 모든 사람들에게 사랑을 받는다.
   (과거) Your car **was towed** away. 네 차가 견인 되어 갔어.
   (미래) You **will be punished**. 너는 벌 받을 거야.
   (현재진행) Spaghetti **is being cooked** by my mother. 스파게티가 엄마에 의해 요리되고 있다.
   (현재완료) Pizza **has been delivered**. 피자가 배달되었다.

# Unit Test

**1.** 각 문장을 수동태 문장으로 바꿔 쓰시오. (시제에 유의)

1. Everybody loves Ellis.

   →_____

2. Snakes eat frogs.

   →_____

3. A mosquito bit me.

   →_____

4. My mother made this cake.

   →_____

5. My boss used me.

   →_____

**2.** 보기의 문장을 괄호안의 지시대로 바꾸시오.

| 보기 | Jinny is loved by everyone. |

1. (의문문)   →_____

2. (과거)   →_____

3. (미래)   →_____

4. (현재완료)   →_____

**3.** 보기와 같이 ( )안의 동사를 적절한 형태로 바꿔 문장을 완성하시오.

| 보기 | Laura <u>was born</u> (bear) in Seattle. |

1. English _____ (speak) in many countries. (현재)

2. Oranges _____ (import) from Florida. (현재)

3. I _____ (invite) to Cathy's birthday party. (과거)

4. A diamond ring _____ (steal) yesterday. (과거)

5. This car _____ (make) in Germany. (과거)

**4.** 우리말과 일치하도록 괄호 안의 단어를 알맞게 배열하시오.

1. 이 빌딩은 100년 전에 지어졌다. (was/ that building/ 100 years ago/ built)

   _____

2. 너는 언제 태어났니? (were/ born/ you/ when/ ?)

   _____

3. 이 케익은 Michael을 위해 만들어졌다. (was/ this cake/ for/ made/ Michael)

   _____

# Writing Pattern Practice

**1.** 「주어 + be동사 + 과거분사 + by 목적어」

Jane은 모두에게 사랑받는다.(everybody) _____

나는 모기에게 물렸다.(a mosquito) _____

이 케익은 엄마에 의해 만들어졌다. _____

**2.** 「주어 + be동사 + 과거분사 + by 목적어」

영어가 많은 나라에서 말해진다. _____

창문이 깨져 있다. _____

그 편지는 중국말로 쓰여져 있었다.(in Chinese) _____

나는 서울에서 태어났다.(bear) _____

로마는 하루아침에 이루어지지 않았다.(build) _____

**3.** 「주어 + am/ are/ is + 과거분사 (+ by 목적어)」 현재형

나는 많은 사람들에게 도움을 받는다.(many people) _____

당신은 여기에 주차하도록 허락되지 않는다.(allow to~) _____

**4.** 「주어 + was/were + 과거분사 (+ by 목적어)」 과거형

너는 언제 태어났니? _____

이 집은 10년 전에 지어졌다. _____

**5.** 「주어 + will/be going to + be+ 과거분사 (+ by 목적어)」 미래형

너는 벌 받을 거야.(punish) _____

그 상점은 9시에 문 닫을 거야. _____

그 회의는 이번 금요일에 열릴 거야.(hold) _____

**6.** 「주어 + am/ are/ is + being+ 과거분사 (+ by 목적어)」 현재진행형

저녁이 만들어지고 있다.(make) _____

그 빵이 구워지고 있다.(bake) _____

그 차가 견인되고 있다.(tow away) _____

**7.** 「주어 + have/has been + 과거분사 (+ by 목적어)」 현재완료형

그 비밀이 오랫동안 지켜졌다.(The secret~, keep) _____

피자가 배달되었다.(deliver) _____

# 38 수동태표현

Grammar
in
Practice

A: Something smells good.

B: A cake is being made by Mary. She will take it to the party.

A: Were you invited to the party, too?

B: Yeah. I'm really looking forward to it.

Grammar
in
Use

1. 수동태의 부정문은 be동사 뒤에 not을 붙인다.
   This movie **is not** liked by young people. 이 영화는 젊은 사람들에게는 인기가 없다.

2. 수동태의 의문문은 be동사 또는 조동사를 맨 앞에 쓴다. 의문사로 시작하는 의문문은 의문사를 맨 앞에 쓴다.
   **Was** it painted by Picasso? 그것은 피카소가 그린 것이니?
   **Will** the thief be caught soon? 그 도둑이 곧 잡힐까?
   **Where** was the child found? 어디에서 그 아이가 발견되었지?

3. 동사구「동사+전치사/부사」는 수동태에서 분리하지 않고 쓴다.
   Jane was **run over** by a truck. Jane은 트럭에 치였다.
   David was **laughed at** by his classmates. David은 반 친구들에게 비웃음 당했다.

4. 조동사가 있는 문장의 수동태는 「조동사+be동사+과거분사」형태로 쓴다.
   This work **can be done** right away. 이 일은 당장 이루어질 수 있다.(끝날 수 있다)
   The car **may be parked** over there. 그 차는 아마 저쪽에 주차되어 있을 거다.

5. 동사에 따라 「by+행위자」자리에 다른 「전치사+명사」가 올 수 있다.
   Look at the mountain. It's **covered with** snow. 저 산을 봐. 눈으로 덮여있다.
   I'**m interested** in sports. 나는 스포츠에 관심 있다.
   **Are** you **satisfied with** your job? 너는 네 일에 만족하니?
   The singer **is known to** everybody. 그 가수는 모두에게 알려져 있다.
   I **was surprised at[or by]** the news. 나는 그 소식에 놀랐다.
   All of us **are pleased with** the result. 우리 모두는 그 결과에 기쁘다.

# Unit Test

**1.** 각 문장을 수동태 문장으로 바꿔 쓰시오.

1. A truck ran over John.

   → _____

2. I should take care of my baby.

   → _____

3. They can deliver the pizza.

   → _____

4. I may do this work.

   → _____

5. A man picked up the baggage.

   → _____

**2.** 다음 문장을 괄호 안의 지시대로 바꾸시오.

1. That song isn't liked by young people. (긍정문) → _____
2. The letter was written in English. (부정문) → _____
3. This room is cleaned every day. (부정문) → _____
4. She was surprised at the news. (의문문) → _____
5. People are interested in movies. (의문문) → _____

**3.** 빈 칸에 알맞은 전치사를 보기에서 골라 써 넣으시오.

| 보기 | at    in    with    to    with |
|------|--------------------------------|

1. The singer is known _____ everybody.
2. Are you interested _____ music?
3. The mountain is covered _____ snow.
4. I'm not satisfied _____ my job.
5. I was surprised _____ the news.

**4.** 우리말과 일치하도록 괄호 안의 단어를 알맞게 배열하시오.

1. 이런 날씨에는 많은 별들이 보일 수 있다. (can / seen/ many stars/ be/ in this weather)

   _____

2. 그 차가 언제 견인 되어 갔니? (towed away/ the car/ was/ when/ ?)

   _____

3. 그 문제는 풀릴 수 없다. (can't / solved/ the problem/ be)

   _____

# Writing Pattern Practice

**1.** 「주어 + be동사 + not + 과거분사(+by목적어)」 – 수동태 부정문

그 영화는 젊은 사람들에게는 인기가 없다. (like) _____

그 편지는 영어로 쓰여 있지 않았다. _____

그것은 이탈리아에서 만들어진 것이 아니다.(과거) _____

그 문제는 풀리지 않았다.(현재완료) (The problem~) _____


**2.** 「(의문사) + be동사 + 주어 + 과거분사 (+by 목적어)?」

「(의문사) + 조동사 + 주어 + be동사과거분사 (+by 목적어)?」 – 수동태 의문문

그것은 피카소가 그린 것이니?(과거) _____

그 도둑이 곧 잡힐까?(the thief) _____

어디에서 그 아이가 발견되었지? _____

언제 그 책이 출판되었지?(that book, publish) _____


**3.** 「주어 + be동사 + <u>과거분사 + 전치사/부사</u> (+by 목적어)」 – 동사구 수동태

Jane은 트럭에 치였다.(run over) _____

David은 반 친구들에게 비웃음 당했다.(laugh at) _____

그 아기는 베이비시터에게 보살핌을 받고 있다.(take care of)(현재진행)

_____


**4.** 「주어 + 조동사 + be동사 + 과거분사 (+by 목적어)」 – 조동사 수동태

이 일은 당장 이루어질 수 있다.(do, right away) _____

그 차는 아마 저쪽에 주차되어 있을 거다.(may) _____


**5.** 「주어 + be동사 + 과거분사 + 전치사 + 명사 (+by 목적어)」– by 목적어 대신 「전치사 + 명사」

저 산은 눈으로 덮여있다.(The mountain~) _____

나는 스포츠에 관심 있다.(be interested in) _____

너는 네 일에 만족하니?(be satisfied with) _____

나는 그 소식에 놀랐다.(과거) _____

우리 모두는 결과에 기쁘다.(All of us, be pleased with)

_____

**1.** 다음 우리말을 영어로 바꿔 쓰시오.

① 그 상점은 6시에 닫았다.                      → _____
② 그 노래는 젊은 사람들에게 사랑받는다.        → _____
③ 그 책은 곧 출판될 것이다.(publish)          → _____
④ 나는 모기에게 물렸다.                        → _____
⑤ 망고는 한국에서 자라지 않는다.(grow)        → _____

**2.** 다음 영어 문장을 우리말로 쓰시오.

① I am never invited to parties.                    → _____
② The problem can be solved.                        → _____
③ Are you interested in music?                      → _____
④ Was it made in the United States?                 → _____
⑤ The baby is being taken care of by a baby-sitter. → _____

**3.** 다음 중 틀린 곳을 바르게 고치시오.

① I born in Hong Kong.                          → _____
② What language spoken in China?               → _____
③ Are oranges grow in Korea?                   → _____
④ The meeting has been cancel.                 → _____
⑤ The thief wasn't catch.                      → _____
⑥ John was run over a car.                     → _____
⑦ Is Spanish speak in Mexico.                  → _____
⑧ Spicy food is love in Thailand.              → _____
⑨ Harry Potter was write by Joan K. Rowling    → _____
⑩ Disneyland has been visit by many people.    → _____

**4.** 둘 중에서 알맞은 것을 골라 동그라미 하시오.

① I'm interested (by/ in) music.
② The cake was made (by/ of) my mother.
③ The spaghetti was cooked (for/ of) David.
④ That movie star is loved (by/ to) everybody.
⑤ Cindy Chow was born (by/ in) Hong Kong.
⑥ Were you surprised (with/ at) the news?
⑦ Are you satisfied (by/ with) your new job?
⑧ English is spoken (by/ in) many countries.
⑨ My wallet was stolen (by/ in) someone.
⑩ The work will be done (by/ of) Mike.

**1.** 빈 칸에 공통으로 들어갈 알맞은 말은?

I'm satisfied _____ my new bike.

The mountain is covered _____ snow.

Are you pleased _____ the result?

① at                    ② with

③ by                    ④ to

⑤ of

**2.** 어법상 맞는 문장을 고르시오.

① How many people were invited to the party?

② French is speak in Quebec.

③ When was the building build?

④ Mr. White was fire by his boss.

⑤ Pancakes are being cook.

**3.** 어법상 틀린 문장을 고르시오.

① A full moon can be seen today.

② The school was founded in 1930.

③ The house will be painted yellow.

④ The problem has been solved.

⑤ The diamond ring wasn't find.

[4-7] 괄호 안에 들어갈 수 있는 말을 고르시오

**4.** Baseball _____ in most countries.

① plays

② is played

③ played

④ will be play

⑤ has played

**5.** Do you know how this word _____ ?

① pronounce

② is pronounced

③ pronounced

④ will be pronounce

⑤ has pronounced

**6.** A: Where were you _____ ?

B: I was born in Seoul.

① bear

② born

③ be born

④ to be born

⑤ bearing

**7.** A lot of people _____ in the accident.

① injure

② injured

③ were injured

④ to be injured

⑤ injuring

**8.** 다음 글을 읽고 빈칸에 차례로 들어갈 알맞은 말을 고르시오.

① fill - check

② filled - checked

③ filled - check

④ fill - checked

⑤ filling- checked

We go to an airport to get on planes. Airports are _____ with airplanes from different countries. Some are waiting to take off, and some are waiting to land. When planes land, they are carefully _____ for safety. Their tires and engines are checked. They are refueled. After everything is checked, new passengers get on.

*take off 이륙하다 *land 착륙하다

# BASIC
# English
# Grammar
## for Speaking & Writing

**1**

머리에 쏙쏙 들어오는
# 정답 및 해설

MENTORS

# BASIC
## English
## Grammar
*for Speaking & Writing*

## 1권

## 정답 및 해설

Chapter 01    문장의 기본개념 —————————— 2

Chapter 02    문장의 종류 ————————————— 3

Chapter 03    문장의 5형식 ———————————— 9

Chapter 04    동사 —————————————————— 12

Chapter 05    시제 —————————————————— 18

Chapter 06    부정사와 동명사 —————————— 22

Chapter 07    분사 —————————————————— 28

Chapter 08    수동태 ————————————————— 30

# Chapter 01 | 문장의 기본개념

## Unit 1_ 문장의 구성

P.14

### Dialogue

A: 생일축하해. 줄 것이 있어.
B: 고마워. 와, 예쁜 모자네!
A: 마음에 들어?
B: 응, 정말 마음에 들어. 네 선물은 항상 나를 행복하게 해.

### Unit Test

**1.**
1. X    2. O    3. X    4. O    5. X

**2.**
1. I                          2. Mary
3. My parents         4. The weather
5. This bicycle

**3.**
9개 (have, lives, takes, lives, studies, lives, likes, wants, miss)

**4.**
1. mathematics       2. Coke
3. cereal                 4. soccer
5. the room

**5.**
1. 주격보어            2. 목적격보어
3. 주격보어            4. 주격보어
5. 목적격보어

### Writing Pattern Practice

**1.**
I work.
My brother studies hard.
My father smokes.
We eat a lot.
They exercise every day.

**2.**
I eat breakfast every day.
Susan studies English hard.
We like movies.

**3.**
I am happy.
You look pretty.
Mary is tired.
The car is expensive.
He always makes me happy.
Call me Liz.

**4.**
Fortunately, the weather is very nice.
I get up at 6.
Try everything possible.
Look at the girl with blonde hair.
We play tennis on the tennis courts.

## Unit 2_ 단어의 종류

P.17

### Dialogue

A: Daniel에 대해서 뭐가 좋아?
B: 음...유머감각이 좋고 나를 많이 웃겨.
A: 어떻게 생겼는데?
B: 꽤 잘생겼어.

### Unit Test

**1.**
1. 전치사    2. 감탄사    3. 동사    4. 접속사
5. 형용사    6. 명사      7. 명사    8. 부사
9. 동사      10. 전치사   11. 형용사  12. 전치사
13. 형용사   14. 접속사   15. 대명사

**2.**
1. I(주어) eat(동사)
2. Jane(주어) exercises(동사)
3. This bag(주어) is(동사)
4. You(주어) look(동사)
5. Tom and I(주어) go(동사)
6. David's family(주어) has(동사)
7. You(주어) have(동사)

### Writing Pattern Practice

**1.**
Anne lives in Canada.
I have a cell phone.
This is my computer.

**2.**
He's my teacher.

2

This is my bag.
They're my friends.

**3.**

I have a girlfriend.
She drives to work.

**4.**

I'm tired.
The weather is nice.
Have a good time.

**5.**

Please listen carefully.
Sally eats a lot.

**6.**

The keys are on the table.
Let's talk about it.

**7.**

Jack is young, but he's smart.
Say yes or no.

**8.**

Wow, your car is great!
Oh, you have a cold!

## REVIEW 1

**1.**

① I / am a little tired.
② Kate and her family / live in Seattle.
③ Cindy and I / are good friends.
④ Steve / goes to bed late every night.
⑤ Your bag / is under the table.
⑥ It / is sunny today.
⑦ Sandra / speaks Spanish and English.
⑧ I / drink tea.
⑨ These shoes / are mine.
⑩ You and your sister / look just like your mother.
⑪ The weather / is really nice.
⑫ John and Mary / stay in China.
⑬ I / have something for you.
⑭ My brothers and I / play tennis on Saturdays.
⑮ Your handwriting / is terrible.

**2.**

① 주어    ② 보어    ③ 동사    ④ 목적어
⑤ 보어    ⑥ 수식어    ⑦ 주어    ⑧ 보어

⑨ 목적어    ⑩ 수식어

## REVIEW 2

1. ⑤      2. ③      3. ⑤      4. ④      5. ⑤
6. ①, ③      7. ①      8. ②      9. ⑤      10. ⑤

**해설**

1. 문장의 기본요소는 주어, 동사, 목적어, 보어, (수식어)이다.
2. eat은 '먹다' 라는 뜻으로 동사로 쓴다.
3. there은 '저기' 라는 뜻으로 부사로 쓴다.
4. carefully는 '조심스럽게' 라는 뜻으로 부사로 쓴다.
5. ouch는 '아야' 라는 뜻으로 감탄사로 쓴다.
6. 전치사 다음에는 명사와 대명사가 올 수 있다.
7. Anne은 고유명사로 명사에 속한다.
8. happy는 '행복한' 이라는 뜻으로 형용사로 쓴다.
9. wow는 놀라움을 나타내는 감탄사이다.
10. ① Easter(부활절) ② Sunday(일요일) ③ holiday(휴일) ④ homes(가정들)은 명사고 ⑤ brings(가져오다)는 동사다.

**해석**

부활절은 매년 다른 일요일이다. 하지만 항상 3월 또는 4월에 있다. 부활절이 국경일은 아니다. 그것은 기독교인들의 종교적 휴일이다. 아이들은 상상의 토끼, 즉 부활절 토끼가 존재한다고 믿는다. 부활절 전날 밤, 부활절 토끼는 많은 집들을 방문한다. 그는 달걀과 사탕이 들어있는 부활절 바구니를 가져다준다.

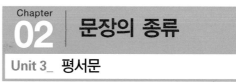

**Chapter 02  문장의 종류**

**Unit 3_ 평서문**

| P.24

### Dialogue

A: 소개 좀 해주세요.
B: 저는 David Whitman이고, Madison 중학교에 다닙니다. 저는 스포츠에 관심이 있습니다. 제가 좋아하는 스포츠는 축구와 수영입니다. 미래에 축구선수가 되고 싶습니다.

### Unit Test

**1.**

3, 5, 6, 7

**2.**

1, 3, 4, 6

**3.**

1. I'm    2. She's    3. can
4. don't    5. live    6. have    7. like

## Writing Pattern Practice

**1.**

I'm from Korea.
You're pretty.
David is in the States.

**2.**

I can speak English.
It will snow.
You must fasten your seatbelt.

**3.**

I like to learn English.
You get up early.
My father smokes.

**4.**

I'm not free.
You aren't fat.
Your sister isn't here.

**5.**

I can't go to the movies.
It won't rain.
People shouldn't drink and drive.

**6.**

Sometimes, I don't like to study.
You don't exercise.
My mother doesn't work.
　＊ 특별히 강조할 때를 제외하면 do/does not을 축약하지 않는 경
　　우는 없다.

## Unit 4_ 명령문과 Let's

| P.27

### Dialogue

A: 오늘밤 영화보자.
B: 좋아. 6시에 데리러와. 알았어?
A: 그래. 이번에는 공포영화보지말자.
B: 알았어. 늦지마.

### Unit Test

**1.**

1. Be happy.    2. Be quiet.

3. Have some more coffee.
4. Take care of my son.
5. Get up early.    6. Don't be late for school.
7. Don't get in the car.
8. Don't play soccer after school.
9. Don't stay up all night.
10. Don't play computer games too much.

**2.**

1. Let's    2 Let's not
3. Let's    4. Let's    5. Let's not

**3.**

1. Have a good trip.
2. Wait for me.
3. Don't be late.
4. Let's see a movie.
5. Turn off your cell phone.
6. Let's not go out.
7. Let's be careful.
8. Don't bother your brother.
9. Let's be quiet.
10. Let's not be absent.

## Writing Pattern Practice

**1.**

Be happy.
Be good.
Come in.
Listen to this music.
Have a good trip.
Wait for me.
Turn off your cell phone.
Help yourself, please.

**2.**

Don't be late.
Don't be sorry.
Don't do that again.
Don't say anything.
Don't bother your brother.
Never give up.

**3.**

Let's go to school.
Let's go out.
Let's study English.
Let's see a movie.
Let's eat dinner.
Let's be careful.

4

Let's be quiet.

**4.**

Let's not go out.
Let's not be absent.
Let's not see a movie.
Let's not cheat.
Let's not talk about it now.

## Unit 5_ 동사로 시작하는 의문문

P.30

### Dialogue

A: 당신은 매일 요리를 합니까?
B: 예, 그래요.
A: 요리를 잘하나요?
B: 예, 그래요.
A: 스파게티를 만들 수 있나요?
B: 물론 할 수 있죠.

### Unit Test

**1.**

1. Is it a nice coat?
2. Is the movie boring?
3. Does Jin go hiking every weekend?
4. Do Tom and John live near here?
5. Can they make it on time?

**2.**

1. You can speak English.
2. Mark is interested in music.
3. It is cold outside.
4. Mr. and Mrs. Smith live in Hawaii.
5. They are sorry for being late.

**3.**

1. Do  2. Does  3. Does  4. Do  5. Do

**4.**

1. Do you have a sister?
2. Is your sister pretty?
3. Do your sister and you go to the same middle school?
4. Do you live with your parents?
5. Do your parents go to church?
6. Is your father strict?
7. Does your mother work?

### Writing Pattern Practice

**1.**

Am I pretty?               Am I fat?
Are you free?              Are you a student?
Are we lost?               Are we late?
Is she a model?            Is he a lawyer?
Is it cold here?           Is this your bag?
Are they nurses?

**2.**

Can you speak English?
Can he swim?
Can Tom cook well?
Can they ski?
Can the children sing well?

**3.**

Do I know you?
Do you cook every day?
Do you have a lot of money?
Does he get up early?
Does she eat breakfast?
Does your brother like English?
Does Jin go hiking every weekend?
Do they go to church every Sunday?
Do Tom and John live near here?

## Unit 6_ 의문사로 시작하는 의문문 1

P.33

### Dialogue

A: 직업이 뭐에요?
B: 저는 교사입니다.
A: 어디에서 근무를 하시나요?
B: 민선고등학교에서 가르칩니다.
A: 몇 시에 출근을 하시나요?
B: 아침 7:30분에 일하러 갑니다.
A: 어떻게 학교까지 가시죠?
B: 차를 몰고 다닙니다.

### Unit Test

**1.**

1. Who  2. Where  3. Where  4. How  5. Why

**2.**

1. Where does David live?
2. Why are you late?
3. What is your favorite color?

4. Where do you exercise?
5. Who do you live with?

**3.**
1. What's your name?-Kathy Kim
2. Who wants to play the role of the princess?-I do.
3. Do I look pretty?-Yes, you do.
4. Does it taste like pizza?-No, it doesn't.
5. Do your parents go to church?-Yes, they do.

**4.**
1. Where do               2. When does
3. Who do                 4 How does
5. What do

## Writing Pattern Practice

**1.**
What's your name?
What's your favorite color?
What can I do?
What do you eat for breakfast?
What does Julie look like?
What do Jack and Molly study?
What should I do?
What bothers you?

**2.**
Where are you?
Where am I?
Where is my coat?
Where do you live?
Where does David exercise?
Where do they have parties?

**3.**
Who's your friend?
Who do you like?
Who do you live with?
Who does Jack love?
Who do they miss?
Who likes chocolate?
Who knows his phone number?
Who has a lot of money?

**4.**
Why are you angry?
Why are they absent?
Why do you study English?
Why does John get up early?
Why does your uncle live in New York?

Why do they work so hard?

**5.**
How are you?
How can I get there?
How do I look?
How do you study English?
How does it taste?
How does Tom get to school?

**6.**
When is your birthday?
When do you study English?
When does Mary eat dinner?
When does the movie begin?
When do they have a meeting?

Unit 7_ 의문사로 시작하는 의문문 2

### Dialogue
A: 좋아하는 명절이 뭐야?
B: 추수감사절.
A: 왜 추수감사절이 가장 좋은데?
B: 왜냐하면 맛있는 칠면조 저녁을 먹을 수 있기 때문이지.

### Unit Test

**1.**
1. 주어역할               2. 목적어역할
3. 주어역할               4. 목적어역할
5. 목적어역할

**2.**
1. Who has a lot of money?
2. Who is late for school?
3. Who isn't at work?
4. Who goes to bed early?
5. Who doesn't like shopping?

**3.**
1. What do you have?
2. What does Mary like?
3. What does Jane need?
4. What do I enjoy?
5. What do Jack and Liz eat for breakfast?

**4.**
1. Where is the phone booth?
2. What color do you like best?

3. Why are you late?
4. When does Mary go to bed?
5. How is your father?
6. Which doctor do you want to see?

## Writing Pattern Practice

**1.**

Who likes you?
Who wants to eat ice cream?
Who will come to the party?

**2.**

Who do you like?
Who does she want to invite?

**3.**

What bothers you?
What makes him tired?

**4.**

What do you eat for dinner?
What does that mean?
What does she want for Christmas?

**5.**

Which has a pocket?

**6.**

Which do you want to buy?
Which does he prefer?

**7.**

Why do you get up so early?
When do they get off work?

**8.**

What day do you have a meeting?
Which color do you prefer, pink or purple?

## Unit 8_ 부정의문문과 부가의문문

P.40

### Dialogue

A: 저 소녀를 봐, 정말 예쁘지 않니?
B: 맞아. 내 스타일이야.
A: 너랑 같은 중학교 다니지, 그렇지 않니?
B: 그런 것 같아.

### Unit Test

**1.**

1. Can't you swim?
2. Doesn't Harry like hiking?
3. Isn't this your hat?
4. Isn't he your roommate?
5. Aren't Paul and Jack close friends?

**2.**

1. Isn't he a good swimmer?
2. Don't women like shopping?
3. Can't you park here?
4. Don't they live in that apartment?
5. Don't his parents enjoy hiking?

**3.**

1. doesn't he
2. can you
3. aren't you
4. does it
5. aren't they

**4.**

1. Aren't you tired?
2. Doesn't your boyfriend live in Florida?
3. Isn't Nicole from New York?
4. Isn't Jack late for class?
5. Can't I sleep a little longer?

## Writing Pattern Practice

**1.**

Aren't you bored?
Isn't he your roommate?
Isn't the weather nice?
Aren't Nicole and you from New York?

**2.**

Can't I borrow your book?
Can't you stay a little longer?
Can't he give us a ride?
Can't we talk about it later?

**3.**

Don't you get up early?
Doesn't your father smoke?
Doesn't Sally work?
Don't they like music?

**4.**

You are sick, aren't you?
The weather is nice, isn't it?
Mary isn't at home, is she?
Gary and you are friends, aren't you?

**5.**

You can come to my birthday party, can't you?
Jane can't be here on time, can she?
Tom and you can stay with me, can't you?

## 6.

You like playing soccer, don't you?
Mary doesn't like math, does she?
They wear school uniforms, don't they?

## Unit 9_ 감탄문

P.43

### Dialogue

A: 멋진 자전거다!
B: 삼촌이 내게 사주셨어.
A: 우리 내일 자전거 타러 가자.
B: 좋아.

### Unit Test

**1.**
1. What　　2. How　　3. How　　4. What
5. How　　6. What　　7. What　　8. How
9. What　　10. How

**2.**
1. a touching movie　　2. a pretty girl
3. beautiful flowers　　4. cute
5. interesting

**3.**
1. What a small world!
2. What a beautiful day!
3. How lovely the baby is!
4. What a pity!
5. How kind he is!
6. What a long day!
7. What nice shoes!

### Writing Pattern Practice

**1.**
How beautiful you are!
How exciting the game is!
How boring the movie was!
How kind he is!
How tall the models are!

**2.**
How fast she ran!
How wonderfully they sang!

## 3.

What a great bike it is!
What pretty flowers they are!
What a great car you have!
What a nice bike it is!
What great students you are!
What expensive cars they are!
What a small world it is!
What a beautiful day it is!

## 4.

What a surprise!
What a shame!
What a play!
What a day!
What a pity!

## REVIEW I

**1.**
① gives → give　　　② sees → see
③ being → be　　　④ Do → Does
⑤ swims → swim　　⑥ Do → Does
⑦ eat → eats　　　⑧ starts → start
⑨ my backpack is → is my backpack
⑩ goes → go

**해설**
① 「Never+동사원형」은 '절대 ~하지마라' 이다.
② 「Let's not+동사원형」은 '~하지말자' 이다.
③ 「Don't+동사원형」은 '~하지마라' 이다.
④ 「Does+she/he/it+동사원형?」은 '~하니?' 이다.
⑤ 조동사가 들어간 문장의 의문문의 구조는 「조동사+주어+동사원형?」이다.
⑥ 일반동사가 들어간 문장의 주어가 3인칭 단수일 경우 구조는 「Does+she/he/it+동사원형?」이다.
⑦ '누가 ~하니?' 는 「Who+동사(e)s ~?」이다.
⑧ '~하지 않니?' 는 주어가 3인칭 단수일 경우 구조는 「Doesn't+she/he/it+동사원형?」이다.
⑨ 「Where+be동사+주어?」는 '~가 어디있니?' 이다.
⑩ '어떻게 ~하니?' 는 주어가 3인칭 단수 일 경우 구조는 「How does+she/he/it+동사원형?」이다.

**2.**
① Let's not be late.
② Where will they have a party?
③ How was the movie?
④ Don't you do your homework every day?
⑤ Jack can swim, can't he?

**3.**

① 냄새가 좋지 않니?

② 누가 Charlie와 머물고 싶니?

③ 너의 부모님은 부산에 사시지, 그렇지 않니?

④ 정말 예쁜 스커트구나!

⑤ 정말 그 영화는 지루했다!

**4.**

① Am I late for work?

② Is Janet raising two kittens?

③ Don't you stay up late?

④ He practices English every day.

⑤ What beautiful hair you have!

⑥ How exciting the concert was!

⑦ Brush your teeth.

⑧ Don't drink too much.

## REVIEW 2

1. ④    2. ④    3. ①, ②    4. ② 5. ④

6. ③    7. try, Do, know

**해설**

1. ① 감탄문 ② 의문문 ③ 명령문 ⑤ 의문문

2. ① Don't late.→Don't be late.

  ② Let's not going there.→Let's not go there.

  ③ How can I getting to the airport? → How can I get to the airport?

  ⑤ Do she know the truth? → Does she know the truth?

3. what은 문장 안에서 주로 의문대명사나 의문형용사역할을 한다.

4. 보기의 who는 주어역할을 한다.

  ① who-전치사의 목적어역할

  ③ who-목적어역할

  ④ who-목적어역할

  ⑤ who-전치사의 목적어

5. ④주어가 they이므로 Isn't 를 Aren't로 고쳐야 한다.

6. 빈칸에 각각 들어갈 말은 ① isn't she? ② is she? ④ doesn't she? ⑤ do they? 이다.

7. '~하지마라' 는 「Don't+동사원형」이고 일반동사가 있는 문장의 의문문은 주어가 you 일 경우 「Do+you+동사원형?」을 쓴다.

**해석**

중국의 많은 사람들은 만리장성을 따라서 걷곤 합니다. 하지만 전체를 따라 걸으려는 시도는 하지 마십시오. 너무 깁니다. 당신은 그 길이를 아십니까? 로스엔젤레스에서 뉴욕까지 4000km를 걷는다고 상상해보십시오. 만리

장성은 그것보다 훨씬 깁니다. 6000km 이상입니다.

# Chapter 03 | 문장의 5형식

## Unit 10_ 1형식 2형식

P.50

### Dialogue

A: 나 어때 보여?

B: 오늘 달라 보인다. 머리잘랐구나, 그렇지?

A: 응, 그래.

B: 전보다 훨씬 젊어 보여.

### Unit Test

**1.**

1. 1형식   2. 1형식   3. 1형식   4. 2형식   5. 2형식

6. 2형식   7. 1형식   8. 1형식   9. 1형식   10. 2형식

**2.**

become, be, sound, feel

**3.**

1. I exercise everyday.

2. You look tired.

3. I'll become a teacher.

4. The juice is in the fridge.

5. I was at the party last night.

6. My father smokes a lot.

7. Does it taste good?

8. James drives to work.

9. Does it sound good?

10. Is that singer famous?

### Writing Pattern Practice

**1.**

The sun rises in the east.

Jane works.

My mother cooks.

There are a lot of people here.

**2.**

I am tall.

Susan is very tired.

They are nurses.

**3.**

You look different today.

You look very tired.
Something smells bad.
The soup smells good.
Does it taste good?
It tastes terrific.
It sounds good.
The fur coat feels soft.
It doesn't feel good.
They seem kind.

**4.**

I'll become a doctor.
Susan became a singer.
I got hungry.
Laura got bored.
The leaves turned red.
It grew dark.

## Unit 11_ 3형식

P.53

### Dialogue

A: 이번 주말에 뭐 할 거니?
B: TV로 야구경기 볼 거야. 너는?
A: 영화 보러 갈 것 같아.
B: 좋겠다.

### Unit Test

**1.**

1. 3형식  2. 1형식  3. 1형식  4. 3형식  5. 2형식
6. 1형식  7. 3형식  8. 3형식  9. 1형식  10. 3형식

**2.**

1. a coat.                     2. three languages
3. how to say this      4. dinner
5. to travel                  6. that I'm stupid
7. that money is not everything

**3.**

1. He enjoys swimming.
2. Most people eat too much fast food.
3. Do you know how to make spaghetti?
4. I know what your name is.
5. Do you think that money is important?

### Writing Pattern Practice

**1.**

I have a car.
I like apples.

You're wearing a hat.
Janet speaks three languages.
Most people eat too much meat.

**2.**

Yes, I like them very much.
No, I didn't bring it.

**3.**

I finished working.
Neil enjoys swimming.
Would you mind opening the window?

**4.**

I want to go on a diet.
I decided to move to New York.
Henry would like to eat out.

**5.**

I learned how to use this machine.
Do you know where to go?

**6.**

I hope that you have a great time.
I want to know if he likes me.
I want to know what her phone number is.
I think that I will see a movie this weekend.

## Unit 12_ 4형식

P.56

### Dialogue

A: 마실 것 좀 가져다줘.
B: 알았어. 오렌지주스 가져다줄게.
A: 커피 마시고 싶은데. 좀 만들어 줄래?
B: 물론이지.

### Unit Test

**1.**

1. 4형식  2. 3형식  3. 3형식  4. 1형식  5. 2형식
6. 4형식  7. 4형식  8. 3형식  9. 4형식  10. 4형식

**2.**

1. Can you lend some money to me?
2. Pass the salt to me, please.
3. Tell a funny story to me.
4. I bought this watch for you.
5. Can you give the books to her?
6. My girlfriend wrote a letter to me.
7. John made some coffee for me.

**3.**

1. Can you lend me 20 dollars?
2. I'll buy you a present.
3. I showed the police officer my driver's license.

## Writing Pattern Practice

**1.**

I gave him a book.
My friend sent me a postcard.
The students asked me some questions.
Would you lend me a pen?
Grandma told me a story.
A man showed me the way to the bank.
She made her daughter a new dress.
Buy me dinner.
Mrs. White teaches us English.
Sue writes him a letter every week.
Please get me some water.
I asked her what to do next.

**2.**

She told a funny story to us.
Lend some money to me.
He taught English to me.
I gave a book to him.
Send it to me.

**3.**

My boyfriend bought a ring for me.
She got some water for me.
I made some coffee for my uncle.

## Unit 13_ 5형식

P.59

### Dialogue

A: 오늘 좋아 보이는데.
B: 파마 했어.
A: 더 예뻐 보인다.
B: 정말? 고마워.

### Unit Test

**1.**

1. 4형식  2. 5형식  3. 5형식  4. 5형식  5. 1형식
6. 2형식  7. 5형식  8. 3형식  9. 5형식  10. 4형식

**2.**

1. dance  2. smile  3. wash  4. go  5. fight

**3.**

1. Richard always makes me happy.
2. Did you see me dance?
3. My mother had me clean up the room.
4. I watched the baby sleeping.
5. People call him Mr. Perfect.
6. I found him to be a liar.
7. Let me introduce myself.

## Writing Pattern Practice

**1.**

I saw you doze/dozing.
Did you see Lisa cheat/cheating?
I like to watch you dance/dancing.
People watched me sing/singing.
I felt Sally cry/crying.
I felt something move/moving.
I heard them fight/fighting.
Did you hear him go out/going out?

**2.**

You always make me smile.
Did I make you feel tired?
I had my son do the laundry.
Please let me go.
Let me introduce myself.

**3.**

Call me Katie.
People call him a fool.
I named the dog Mary.
Who named you Christine?

**4.**

I found Mike nice.
Did you find Cindy a liar?

**5.**

Coffee keeps me awake.
I'm sorry to keep you waiting.

**6.**

Do you want me to vacuum the floor?
I want you to be a singer.

## REVIEW I

**1.**

① 1형식  ② 5형식  ③ 4형식  ④ 3형식

⑤ 2형식   ⑥ 3형식   ⑦ 5형식   ⑧ 2형식
⑨ 3형식   ⑩ 3형식   ⑪ 4형식   ⑫ 5형식
⑬ 1형식   ⑭ 2형식   ⑮ 5형식

## 2.

① tired              ② interesting
③ happy             ④ soft
⑤ eating            ⑥ playing
⑦ to                ⑧ to
⑨ for               ⑩ for

## 3.

① one of my friends   ② to know, if he will leave
for Florida.
③ me                ④ to leave
⑤ Susie

## REVIEW 2

1. ④   2. ①   3. ③   4. ①
5. ④   6. ③   7. ②   8. ③

**해설**

1. 부사구란 두개이상의 단어가 모여서 문장 안에서
   부사역할을 하는 것이다.
   **예** Once upon a time, there lived an old king.
   I came here to see you.
   My church stands on the hill.
   The movie starts at 4.
   부사나 부사절은 형식에 영향을 미치지 않는다.
2. smell은 '~냄새가 나다' 라는 감각동사로 쓰일 경
   우 2형식 문장을 만든다.
3. ③번 문장에서 he is a single은 that이 생략된 목
   적절이다.
4. ①번 문장은 'Sally는 나에게 편지를 썼다' 라는 뜻
   으로 간접목적어 me와 직접목적어 letter를 쓴 4형
   식 구조다.
5. ④번 문장은 사역동사를 쓴「let+목적어+목적어보
   어」구조이다.
6. 빈칸은 간접목적어 자리이므로 인칭대명사의 목적
   격이 들어가야 한다.
7. want는 5형식문장에서 '~가 …하기를 원한다' 라
   는 뜻으로 쓰면서 to 부정사를 목적격보어로 취한다.
8. ③번 문장은 '그것은 우리를 행복하고 신나게 만든
   다' 라는 뜻으로 목적어 us와 목적격보어 feel
   happy and excited를 쓴 5형식 구조다.

**해석**

많은 사람들은 그들의 사랑을 초콜릿을 주는 것으로

보여줍니다. 그들은 초콜릿을 사랑의 어떤 상징으로
생각합니다.
그런데 말이죠. 초콜릿이 정말 사랑과 연관될 수도 있
습니다. 연구원들은 초콜릿을 먹는 것이 우리 뇌에 어
떤 작용을 일으킨다는 것을 알아냈습니다. 그것은 우
리를 행복하고 신나게 만들어 줍니다. 초콜릿은 우리
가 누군가를 사랑할 때와 같은 감정을 생성합니다.
그러므로, 지금 외로우신가요? 남자친구나 여자친구
가 없으세요? 그럼 초콜릿을 드세요.

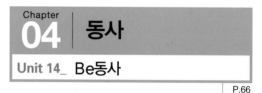

## Chapter 04 | 동사

### Unit 14_ Be동사

| P.66

### Dialogue

A: 이름이 뭐예요?
B: 제 이름은 Jack입니다.
A: 미국에서 오셨나요?
B: 아니오. 캐나다에서 왔어요.
A: 결혼 하셨어요?
B: 예, 했어요. 제 아내는 영어교사예요.

### Unit Test

**1.**
1. am   2. is   3. is   4. are   5. are

**2.**
1. is Jack              2. is not
3. is from Canada       4. is
5. is an English teacher

**3.**
1. is hungry            2. are married
3. is upstairs

**4.**
1. is nice              2. aren't fun
3. isn't diligent       4. are Australian
5. isn't poor           6. is ugly
7. is six               8. are heavy
9. is upstairs          10. is closed

### Writing Pattern Practice

**1.**
I'm tired today.
You're pretty.

You're very diligent.
Sally is afraid of dogs.
It's eight thirty. You're late again.

**2.**

I'm not hungry.
She isn't sad.
The weather isn't nice today.
We aren't healthy.

**3.**

I'm a student.
You're a fool.
They're lawyers.
Tom and I are close friends.

**4.**

I'm not fat.
You aren't a genius.
He isn't a police officer.
Those people aren't American.

**5.**

I'm upstairs.
You're home.
He's inside.
Tom and Jerry are outside.
Nobody's here.

**6.**

I'm not home.
John isn't downstairs.
Tom isn't here.
They aren't outside.

## Unit 15_ 일반동사

P.69

### Dialogue

A: 커피 드실래요?
B: 아니 됐어요. 커피는 안 마셔요. 차 좀 마실께요.
Q: 그녀는 커피를 좋아해요?
A: 아니오, 그녀는 커피 안 마셔요.
Q: 그녀는 무엇을 마시기를 원해요?
A: 그녀는 차를 마시기를 원해요.

### Unit Test

**1.**

1. listens  2. likes  3. love  4. rains  5. do

**2.**

1. am believing → believe
2. is belonging → belongs
3. are you preferring → do you prefer
4. is wanting → wants
5. is understanding → understands
6. am hating → hate
7. Is Kate liking → Does Kate like
8. is knowing → knows
9. are seeming → seem
10. is fitting→ fits

**3.**

works, likes, cost, hope, achieve

**4.**

1. I don't play the violin very well.
2. My sister doesn't play the piano very well.
3. John doesn't hate to cook.
4. You don't work very hard.
5. My parents don't enjoy playing golf.

### Writing Pattern Practice

**1.**

I like soccer.
I know his phone number.
You have a girlfriend.
We go jogging every day.
They always eat breakfast.

**2.**

Everybody likes music.
Nobody cares.
Cindy walks her dog every day.
My father drinks coffee a lot.
James likes movies.
It snows a lot in the winter.
It rains a lot on Jeju Island.

**3.**

I don't exercise.
You don't eat vegetables.
We don't watch television very often.
They don't have much money.
My parents don't sleep in.

**4.**

Sally doesn't eat meat.
My brother doesn't drink Coke.
It doesn't snow much in Tokyo.

The television doesn't work.

## Unit 16_ 조동사 can/could

P.72

### Dialogue

A: 무엇을 도와드릴까요?
B: 10달러 지폐좀 바꿔주실래요?
A: 물론이죠. 여기있어요.

### Unit Test

**1.**

1. He can swim.
2. He can ride a horse
3. He can't drive.
4. He can ski.

**2.**

1. Can, help
2. can taste
3. can't come
4. can speak
5. can't tell

**3.**

1. Can I sit here?
2. You can park here.
3. It can't be true.
4. Could I have a cup of coffee?
5. Could I have your name?
6. I couldn't say a word.
7. My mother can't speak English.

### Writing Pattern Practice

**1.**

I can ski.
He can speak French very well.
I can't make spaghetti.

**2.**

Can I park here?
Can I ask your name?
Can I use the phone?
You can sit here.
You can swim in the pool.

**3.**

It can't be true.
It can't be possible.
He can't be married.

**4.**

I couldn't say a word.

Ted couldn't attend the meeting.
We couldn't sleep well.

**5.**

I could go to the party.
He could be at home.
It could be Cathy's bag.

**6.**

Could you help me?
Could you give me a ride home?
Could you change a ten-dollar bill?

## Unit 17_ 조동사 may/might

P.75

### Dialogue

A: 질문 하나 해도 될까요?
B: 물론이죠.
A: 여기서 White 박사님과 만나기로 했는데요. 어떻게 만나뵐 수 있을까요?
B: 지금 아마 회의실에 계실 거예요.

### Unit Test

**1.**

1. May
2. may
3. may not

**2.**

1. I might see a movie.
2. Leo might be here soon.
3. Mark might be at home.
4. It might snow this afternoon.
5. There might be some misunderstanding.

**3.**

1. I might not be home until tomorrow.
2. It might not rain tomorrow.
3. There might not be anybody in there.
4. Susan might not come back to Korea.
5. It might not be cold tonight.

### Writing Pattern Practice

**1.**

May I take your order?
May I ask a question?
May I leave a message?
May I sit here?
May I have your name?

14

You may use my pen.
You may park here.
You may use my phone.
You may not smoke here.

**2.**
I may go to Japan.
I may be absent.
You may be tired.
Your coat may be in the closet.
Jack may come here.
They may stay here for a week.

**3.**
I might go to Europe.
I might be late.
You might be bored.
You glasses might be on the desk.
Jenny might be in her room.
It might snow tomorrow.
It might be true.
They might get here tomorrow.
There might be some milk in the fridge.

## Unit 18_ 조동사 will/would

P.78

### Dialogue

A: 이 카트가 망가졌어요. 좀 도와 주실래요?
B: 물론이죠. 들어다 드릴께요.

*ma' am : 성인 여자를 높여서 부르는 말로 굳이 해석할 필요 없다.

### Unit Test

**1.**
1. won't   2. will   3. will   4. will   5. won't

**2.**
1. Will you hand it to me? - Will you buy me some flowers?
2. The door won't open. - This car won't move.
3. Will you come to the meeting? - I will eat a sandwich for lunch.
4. This hat will be in the closet. - That will be 10 dollars each.
5. Will you drink some wine? - Will you have some cake?

**3.**
1. Would you like to go out to eat ?

2. Would you like to eat some cake?
3. Would you like to eat some ice cream?
4. Would you like to go out for a walk?
5. Would you like to play tennis?

**4.**
1. 'd rather          2. 'd rather not
3. 'd rather          4. 'd rather not
5. 'd rather

### Writing Pattern Practice

**1.**
I will eat spaghetti for lunch.
I will go home now.
Sally won't be late.

**2.**
He won't listen to me.
The window won't open.
My ring won't come off.

**3.**
Will you have some Coke?
Will you do me a favor?

**4.**
That will be the most popular movie this summer.
That will be $20.
That will be a great painting.

**5.**
When I was young, I would study hard.
He would often go swimming.

**6.**
Would you have dinner with me?
Would you spell that?

**7.**
I'd like to eat out.
Would you like some tea?
Would you like to go for a walk?

**8.**
I'd rather stay home.
I'd rather not go there.
Would you rather take a taxi?

## Unit 19_ 조동사 shall/should/had better

P.81

### Dialogue

A: 우리 내일 일 끝내도 될까요?
B: 안돼. 오늘 마쳐야해. 서둘러야해.
A: 커피마시면서 조금 쉬었다하죠, 그럴래요?
B: 아니, 시간이 별로 없어. 그냥 계속 일하지.

### Unit Test

**1.**

| | |
|---|---|
| 1. should | 2. should |
| 3. shouldn't | 4. shouldn't |
| 5. shouldn't | 6. should |
| 7. shouldn't | 8. shouldn't |
| 9. shouldn't | 10. should |

**2.**

| | |
|---|---|
| 1. 'd better | 2. 'd better not |
| 3. 'd better not | 4. 'd better |
| 5. 'd better | |

**3.**

1. Shall we take a break?
2. You should not lie.
3. She should see a doctor.
4. You had better be quiet.
5. You had better not cry.

### Writing Pattern Practice

**1.**

Shall I sit here?
Shall I close the window?
Shall we dance?
Shall we talk about it later?

**2.**

Let's go for a walk, shall we?
Let's eat dinner, shall we?
Let's take a break, shall we?
Let's leave now, shall we?

**3.**

You should see a doctor.
You should be there on time.
You shouldn't watch too much TV.
Should I dress up?

**4.**

You should be tired.
Tim should be at his office at this hour.
The remote control should be next to the television.

**5.**

You'd better watch out.
You'd better take the subway.
You'd better not be absent.
You'd better not be late.
You'd better not cry.

## Unit 20_ 조동사 must/ have to/ have got to

P.84

### Dialogue

A: 다이어트 해야겠어. 나 60kg 넘게 나가.
B: 아니야. 그럴 필요 없어, 딱 좋은 것 같은데.
A: 진심이야?
B: 물론이지.

### Unit Test

**1.**

| | |
|---|---|
| 1. must not | 2. must not |
| 3. must | 4. must not |
| 5. must not | 6. must |

**2.**

1. You must not stay here.
2. I have to get up early.
3. Jack cannot be at work.
4. It must be true.
5. You must stay up all night.

**3.**

1. You have got to wait here.
2. Must I finish this by tomorrow?
3. Does Kim have to work on Saturdays?

### Writing Pattern Practice

**1.**

You must fasten your seatbelt.
Must we study English?

**2.**

You must not drink and drive.
You must not park here.

**3.**

It must be true.

Jack must be in his room.

You must weigh over 50kg.

There must be a lot of people here on Friday night.

**4.**

Gary can't be married.

It can't be true.

**5.**

I have to go right now.

Jin has to study.

Do you really have to leave now?

We had to attend the meeting.

Susie will have to go and see Mrs. Wilson.

**6.**

You don't have to wait for me.

You didn't have to pay for it.

**7.**

You've got to do your homework.

I've got to go.

Have you got to go now?

**8.**

You've got to be joking.

That bag has got to be expensive.

James has got to be at home.

## REVIEW 1

**1.**

① like → likes

② rain → rains

③ 'm knowing → know

④ Are you liking → Do you like

⑤ 're understanding → understand

⑥ don't → doesn't

⑦ doesn't → don't

⑧ speaks → speak

⑨ is → be

⑩ 'd like to → 'd like

**해설**

**1.**

① everybody는 항상 단수 취급한다.

② 주어가 3인칭 단수인 현재형 문장은 동사원형에 -

(e)s를 붙인다.

③ know는 진행형을 쓸 수 없는 동사다.

④ like는 진행형을 쓸 수 없는 동사다.

⑤ understand는 진행형을 쓸 수 없는 동사다.

⑥ 주어가 3인칭단수인 현재형문장의 부정은 「주어 +doesn't+동사원형」이다.

⑦ 주어가 복수일 때 현재형문장의 부정은 「주어 +don't+동사원형」이다.

⑧ 조동사 다음에는 항상 동사원형이 와야한다.

⑨ 조동사 다음에는 항상 동사원형이 와야한다.

⑩ 「'd like to+동사원형」이고「'd like+명사」임을 유의한다.

**2.**

① John is downstairs.

② They are doctors.

③ I'd rather take a taxi.

④ The window won't open.

⑤ You'd better not be absent.

**3.**

① 너는 여기에 주차해도 좋아.

② 그것은 20불입니다.

③ 그것이 가능할 리 없다.

④ 너는 50Kg 이상 나감에 틀림없다.

⑤ 너는 농담하고 있음에 틀림없다.

**4.**

① John isn't upstairs.

② We don't watch television often.

③ You'd better not go there.

④ I can't make spaghetti.

⑤ We are tired.

⑥ You must turn left here.

⑦ It could be true.

⑧ I'd rather stay here.

## REVIEW 2

1. ④     2. ④     3. ④     4. ⑤     5. ④     6. ①

7. 그들이 그것을 가지고 있음에 틀림없다.

**해설**

1. ① am→ are       ② walk→ walks
   ③ plays→ play  ⑤ will you?→ shall we?

2. ④ snows→ snow

3. ④번은 can이 능력의 뜻이고 나머지는 허락의 뜻이다.

4. ⑤번은 must가 의무/금지의 뜻이고 나머지는 강한 추측의 뜻이 된다.

5. must be(강한추측)의 부정은 can't be를 써야 한다.
6. have to가 들어있는 문장의 의문문은 「Do/Does+ 주어+have to+동사원형?」이다.
7. must는 '꼭 ~을 해야 한다' 와 '~임에 틀림없다' 의 두 뜻으로 주로 쓰이는데 문맥상 강한 추측으로 쓰였음을 알 수 있다.

**해석**

한국 사람들은 인스턴트 국수를 매우 좋아합니다. 라면이라는 인스턴트 국수는 세계적으로 인기입니다. 그들이 얼마나 라면을 좋아하는지 아십니까? 한국 가게에서는 100가지 이상의 라면을 살 수 있습니다. 소고기나 야채라면, 닭이나 오징어 라면, 그리고 맵거나 순한 맛의 라면을 찾을 수 있습니다. 두껍거나 얇은 라면을 찾을 수 있습니다. 어떤 종류의 라면을 먹기를 원하든지 한국에는 틀림없이 있을 것입니다.

# Chapter 04 | 시제

## Unit 21_ 현재시제

### Dialogue

A: 네 남자친구에 대해 얘기해봐.
B: 잘 생기고 모두에게 친절해. 항상 다른 사람들을 행복하게 만들고 친구들도 많아.

### Unit Test

**1.**

come→comes  go→goes  eat→eats
drink→drinks  get→gets  take→takes
have→has  dream→dreams  sleep→sleeps
sit→sits  stand→stands  say→says
pay→pays  buy→buys  cry→cries

**2.**

|  | /s/ | /z/ | /iz/ |
|---|---|---|---|
| eats | o | | |
| likes | o | | |
| comes | | o | |
| kisses | | | o |
| sleeps | o | | |
| buys | | o | |
| finishes | | | o |
| goes | | o | |
| wants | o | | |
| listens | | o | |

**3.**

speaks, takes, listens, works, has, practices, speaks, studies.

**4.**

1. Mark speaks five languages.
2. Water boils at 100℃
3. I walk to school.
4. The sun sets in the west.
5. You speak English well.

## Writing Pattern Practice

**1.**

I get up early.
I come from Canada.
You have a lot of money.
We live in Hawaii.
We go to the same school.
They speak English well.
Tom and Mary go to church.

**2.**

I don't have much money.
I don't exercise.
You don't have a girlfriend.
You don't study hard.
We don't eat meat.
We don't work.
They don't come from Canada.
My parents don't live in Korea.

**3.**

Jane takes a shower every day.
Jack drives to work every day.
Water freezes at 0℃.
Water boils at 100℃.
That store opens at 9.
The sun rises in the east.

**4.**

Cindy doesn't eat pork.
David doesn't exercise.
My sister doesn't drink Coke.
It doesn't snow in Hawaii.

## Unit 22_ 현재진행시제

### Dialogue

A: 너희 가족은 지금 무엇을 하고 있니?

B: 우리 아버지는 커피를 마시고 계셔. 아버지는 커피를 좋아하시거든. 어머니는 점심으로 오믈렛을 만들고 계셔. 어머니는 요리를 정말 잘 하시지. 그리고 우리 형은 TV를 보고 있어. 그는 TV를 정말 좋아해.

## Unit Test

**1.**

| | |
|---|---|
| vacuum → vacuuming | cry → crying |
| snow → snowing | live → living |
| go → going | stop → stopping |
| swim → swimming | open → opening |
| rain → raining | die → dying |
| begin → beginning | play → playing |

**2.**
1. is taking some pictures.
2. is eating some ice cream.
3. is walking the dog.
4. is singing.
5. are playing badminton.

**3.**
1. She is taking a shower.
2. Cindy likes coffee.
3. I'm not watching it now.
4. I'm looking for my bag.
5. He plays soccer very often.

## Writing Pattern Practice

**1.**

I'm taking a shower.
I'm going to school.
My brother is talking on the phone.
Jim is smoking.
It's snowing.
The sun is shining.
My mother and I are cleaning the house.
We're eating breakfast.
They're playing badminton.

**2.**

I'm not sleeping.
I'm not talking on the phone.
You aren't doing your homework.
You aren't exercising.
Terry isn't cleaning his room.
Kathy isn't bothering her brother.
It isn't raining.

They aren't having a party.

**3.**
Am I bothering you?
Are you eating breakfast?
Are you taking a shower?
Is Monica listening to the radio?
Is John watching TV?
Is it raining?
Are they sweeping the floor?
Are they fighting?

## Unit 23_ 과거시제
P.98

### Dialogue

A: 휴가 어땠니?
B: 정말 좋았어.
A: 뭐했는데?
B: 우리 가족과 함께 제주도를 갔었어.
우리는 해변에 갔었는데, 정말 재미있었어.

## Unit Test

**1.**

| | | |
|---|---|---|
| 1. woke up | 2. got up | 3. washed |
| 4. brushed | 5. took off | 6. ate |
| 7. put on | 8. went | 9. studied |
| 10. had | 11. played | 12. came |
| 13. drank | 14. watched | 15. told |
| 16. slept | | |

**2.**
went, left, arrived, swam, watched, were, had, came

**3.**

| | |
|---|---|
| 1. snowed | 2. washed |
| 3. flew | 4. ate |
| 5. worked | |

## Writing Pattern Practice

**1.**
I was with my friends.
You were fat.
Daniel was late this morning.
We were in Busan last week.

**2.**
I wasn't with Ted last night.

You weren't thin.
David wasn't absent.
It wasn't hot yesterday.
They weren't here.

**3.**
Was I late?
Were you at the party?
Was it sunny yesterday?
Were they tired?

**4.**
I saw a movie with my friends.
You bought a new coat.
Liz went shopping.
We did our homework.
My parents left for Japan.

**5.**
I didn't do my homework.
I didn't sleep well last night.
You didn't clean your room.
It didn't rain.
We didn't get up early.

**6.**
Did I bother you?
Did I wake you?
Did you brush your teeth?
Did Julia call you last night?

## Unit 24_ 과거진행시제

| P.102

### Dialogue

(형사) 어젯밤 11시 뭐하고 계셨습니까?
(혐의자1) 차 몰고 집에 가고 있었어요.
(혐의자2) 자고 있었어요.

### Unit Test

**1.**
1. I was watching a movie.
2. Jinny was driving home.
3. My uncle was riding a horse.
4. We were doing our homework.
5. My daughter was talking on the phone.

**2.**
1. was having breakfast.
2. was driving to work.
3. was working.

**3.**
1. I was wearing a hat.
2. The girl was eating ice cream.
3. It was raining.
4. We were living in Italy.
5. Leo and I were playing tennis.

### Writing Pattern Practice

**1.**
I was thinking about you.
I was wearing a hat.
You were sleeping.
Molly was eating pizza for lunch.
My friends and I were having a party.
Jack was vacuuming the floor.
Leo and I were playing tennis.
It was snowing.

**2.**
I wasn't studying.
I wasn't thinking about the test.
You weren't exercising.
Tom wasn't cleaning the room.
Kate wasn't bothering her brother.
They weren't having a party.
They weren't waiting for you.

**3.**
Were you eating breakfast?
Were you taking a shower?
Were you looking for this pen?
Was Monica listening to the radio?
Was Jack watching TV?
Was the girl eating ice cream?
Was it raining?
Were they fighting?

## Unit 25_ 현재완료시제

| P.105

### Dialogue

A: 디즈니랜드 가봤니?
B: 아니, 하지만 사진에서 본 적있어. 정말 크지?
A: 응, 우리 가족은 모두 둘러보는데 일주일 걸렸어.

## Unit Test

**1.**

1. have just finished
2. have been
3. has waited for you
4. have turned off
5. has rained
6. have been
7. has tried
8. has got
9. have known
10. has been cold

**2.**

1. has left home
2. has bought glasses.
3. has broken his leg

**3.**

1. T
2. F(has begun→began) 또는 (at 3 o'clock 삭제)
3. F('ve finished→finished) 또는 (yesterday 삭제)
4. T        5. T

## Writing Pattern Practice

**1.**

I've just had dinner.
I've already finished my homework.
Jane has just left.
I haven't decided yet.
Have you just got(ten) home?
Has Cindy already left?

**2.**

I've tried Mexican food.
You've seen the movie 'Titanic'.
We've been to Disneyland.
James hasn't tried bungy jumping.
Have you (ever) been to Florida?

**3.**

I've waited for you for an hour.
Ted has worked here for 20 years.
It has rained for a week.
We've known each other for 10 years.
We haven't seen Mr. Kim for a year.
How long has it rained?
How long have you known each other?

**4.**

I've had enough.
I've lost my book.
Janet has gone to the United States.
Nancy has left for New York.
Have you finished your homework?

### Dialogue

A: 이번 금요일 생일파티를 할 거야.
   올거니?
B: 물론, 가야지.
A: 좋아. Jack과 Michael도 온대.

## Unit Test

**1.**

is going to take a shower.
are going to play tennis.
is going to rain.

**2.**

1. will        2. will        3. will        4. will
5. won't       6. will        7. will        8. won't
9. won't       10. will

**3.**

1. It will rain.
2. We will win the game.
3. I am going to eat a sandwich for lunch.
4. Jim is leaving tonight.
5. We aren't going to the party.

## Writing Pattern Practice

**1.**

I'll go to Chicago next week.
I'll miss you.
Mom, I won't let you down.
You'll be fat.
It'll be sunny.
We'll win the game.
What will you do?
Will you come on time?
Will you join us?
Won't you help me get up?

**2.**

I'm going to swim.
I'm not going to eat dinner.
We're going to see a movie tonight.
My aunt is going to have a baby.
What are you going to do?
Are you going to be at home?
Is it going to rain?

**3.**

I'm leaving tonight.

Kate is getting married next week.
David is getting here in an hour.
We aren't going to the party.
What are you doing tonight?
Are you coming tonight?

## REVIEW I

**1.**

① He exercises every day.
② I ate dinner
③ We haven't eaten(=tried) Thai food.
④ Will it rain?
⑤ Are you going to have a party?

**2.**

① 너는 뚱뚱했었어.
② 너는 잠을 자고 있었니?
③ 너는 파리에 가본 적이 있니?
④ 나는 방금 여기에 도착했어.
⑤ 눈이 올까?

**3.**

① take → taking
② Did you your → Did you do your
③ watch → watching
④ sees → see
⑤ be → been

해설

① be동사와 일반동사를 이어서 쓸 수 없다. 진행형은 「주어+be동사+동사-ing」이다. ② 일반동사가 들어간 문장의 과거의문문은 「Did+주어+동사원형?」인데 동사가 빠져있다. ③ be동사와 일반동사를 이어서 쓸 수 없다. 진행형은 「주어+be동사+동사-ing」이다. ④ 조동사가 들어간 문장의 의문문은 「조동사+주어+동사원형?」이다. ⑤ 현재완료 문장의 의문문은 「Have/Has+주어+과거분사?」이다.

**4.**

① Does Sue get up early?
② I didn't lose my keys.
③ We took a vacation.
④ Jane has had lunch.
⑤ Did Shakespeare write many plays?
⑥ I won't go to bed early.
⑦ Are they going to invite Karen?
⑧ I have told him.
⑨ It is going to rain.
⑩ I haven't started my new job.

## REVIEW 2

1. ②   2. ④   3. ①   4. ⑤   5. ②   6. ④
7. ②

해설

1. ① be동사와 일반동사를 이어서 사용할 수 없다.
   ③ 현재완료문장의 의문문은 주어가 3인칭 단수일 경우 「Has+she/he/it+과거분사?」이다.
   ④ be동사와 일반동사를 이어서 사용할 수 없다.
   ⑤ 일반적인 사실을 나타낼 때 항상 현재형문장을 쓴다.
2. ④ 현재진행형시제는 과거부사와 쓰일 수 없다.
3. '다음 주에 그녀는 뉴욕에 가 있을 것이다.' 라는 미래 문장이다.
4. 'Amy는 지난주에 영화를 두 번 보러갔다' 라는 과거 문장이다.
5. 'Richard를 만나봤니, 아니면 내가 너에게 소개해줄까?' 라는 현재완료 문장이다.
6. B가 '전화 통화를 하고 있었어요.' 라고 과거진행형으로 대답을 했으므로 같은 시제로 물어봐야한다.
7. 2000년 전의 발렌타인데이에 대해 설명하고 있으므로 과거형을 써야한다.

해석

2월14일 발렌타인데이에 세계 대부분의 사람들은 사랑을 축하한다. 로마의 젊은 남자와 여자는 2천년 전에 사랑을 축하했다. 하지만 남자와 여자들은 카드, 꽃다발 또는 초콜릿 등을 서로 주고받지 않았다. 여자들은 그들의 이름을 단지 안에 넣고 남자들은 단지 안에서 한 개의 이름을 뽑아내면 그 남자는 1년 동안 그 이름을 가진 여자의 남자친구가 되어야 했다. 다행히도 우리는 더 이상 그렇게 하지 않는다.

---

Chapter **06** | 부정사와 동명사

Unit 27_ 명사 역할을 하는 to 부정사

P.116

## Dialogue

A: 너는 무엇을 하기를 원하니?
B: 나는 테니스를 치고 싶어.
A: 밖에 좀 추운데. 우리 안에서 탁구 치면 어떨까?
B: 좋아.

## Unit Test

**1.**

1. to see
2. not to be
3. to stay
4. to be
5. to rain
6. not to travel
7. to do
8. to be
9. to be
10. to drive

**2.**

1. to eat
2. to drive
3. to ask
4. to be
5. to turn off

**3.**

1. I decided to sell my car.
2. What do you want to do?
3. I tried to do my best.
4. I hate to be late.
5. Jane decided to go to Italy.
6. Would you like to eat a sandwich?
7. Rita hopes to be a singer.

## Writing Pattern Practice

**1.**

It's fun to be with my friends.
It's exciting to learn English.
It's important to exercise every day.
It's difficult to make spaghetti.
It's not easy to catch a taxi here.
It's hard to quit smoking.
It's impossible to get there on time.

**2.**

I want to go bowling.
Tess needs to clean her room.
Jane decided not to leave.
Rita hopes to be a singer.
I'd like to eat spaghetti.
Don't forget to turn off the light.
It started to rain.
I like to eat out.
Jane hates to clean her room.
I tried to do my best.
Would you like to eat a sandwich?

**3.**

My goal is to become a doctor.
I want you to come to my party.
Do you want me to become a singer?
I told you to come on time.
My mother always tells me to study hard.

## Unit 28_ 형용사 역할을 하는 to 부정사

| P.119

### Dialogue

A: 나 목말라.
B: 마실 것 갖다 줄게.
   뭐 원하니?
A: 물을 원해.
B: 여기 있어.

### Unit Test

**1.**

1. 명사
2. 명사
3. 명사
4. 형용사
5. 형용사
6. 형용사
7. 형용사
8. 형용사
9. 명사
10. 명사
11. 명사
12. 명사
13. 명사
14. 명사
15. 형용사

**2.**

1. I need something to eat.
2. You have a lot of things to do.
3. Jane bought some books to read.
4. Bob has no time to sleep.
5. You need a friend to rely on.
6. We had no time to have lunch.
7. They had no time to see a movie.
8. There is something to eat in the fridge.
9. Do you have any homework to finish?
10. I'll get you something to drink.

### Writing Pattern Practice

**1.**

something to do
I have something to do.
something to read
I need something to read.
food to eat
There is no food to eat.
money to spend
He has a lot of money to spend.
friends to meet
I have some friends to meet today.
water to drink
Give me some water to drink.

**2.**

chairs to sit on
There are no chairs to sit on.
a friend to study English with

I need a friend to study English with.
a friend to have lunch with
I want a friend to have lunch with.
something to write with
I need something to write with.
something to write on
Please give me something to write on.
someone to talk to
I need someone to talk to.
a house to live in
Do you have a house to live in?
a roommate to live with
I want a roommate to live with.

## Unit 29_ 부사 역할을 하는 to 부정사

### Dialogue

A: 만나서 반가워요.
B: 나도 만나서 반가워요.
A: 말씀 많이 들었어요.
B: 좋은 얘기였으면 좋겠네요.

### Unit Test

**1.**

| | | | |
|---|---|---|---|
| 1. 부사 | 2. 부사 | 3. 명사 | 4. 형용사 |
| 5. 명사 | 6. 형용사 | 7. 부사 | 8. 부사 |
| 9. 부사 | 10. 부사 | 11. 부사 | 12. 형용사 |
| 13. 형용사 | 14. 명사 | 15. 형용사 | |

**2.**
1. That book was fun to read.
2. I came here to see you.
3. You were lucky to get a new job.
4. I am happy to see you here.
5. She went out to see her friends.
6. You were foolish to say that.
7. Are you waiting to see the doctor?
8. The movie was difficult to understand.
9. I'm working at two jobs to make a lot of money.
10. I turned on the TV to watch the news.

### Writing Pattern Practice

**1.**

I came here to see Henry.
I tried not to be late.
He did his best to win the game.

Mandy went shopping to buy a coat.
Charlie went to Tokyo to learn Japanese.
What do I need to open an account?

**2.**
It's nice to meet you.
It was good to hear from you.
I'm glad to hear the news.
I'm happy to hear that.

**3.**
You were foolish to do something like that.
You must be a genius to solve the problem.
My father was lucky to get a new job.

**4.**
He grew up to be a great singer.
Her mother lived to be eighty.

**5.**
This book was fun to read.
This river is very dangerous to swim in.
That movie was difficult to understand.

## Unit 30_ to 부정사의 의미상 주어

### Dialogue

A: 생일 축하해!
B: 고마워. 내 생일을 기억하다니 다정하구나.
A: 선물을 열어보지 그래?
B: 알았어. 스웨터네. 내가 딱 원했던 거야.

### Unit Test

**1.**

| | | | | |
|---|---|---|---|---|
| 1. you | 2. you | 3. She | 4. me | 5. you |
| 6. them | 7. me | 8. you | 9. her | 10. me |

**2.**

| | | | | |
|---|---|---|---|---|
| 1. of | 2. for | 3. of | 4. for | 5. of |
| 6. of | 7. for | 8. for | | |

**3.**
1. It's kind of you to help me.
2. It's unusual for him to make jokes.
3. Is it possible for you to come here on time?
4. It was careless of him to say that.
5. It's important for her to study hard.

## Writing Pattern Practice

### 1.

These pants are too big for you to wear.
This tea is too hot for me to drink.
It's impossible for him to get up early.
It's difficult for them to come here right away.
It's time for us to go to bed.
It's important for you to be on time.
This vacuum cleaner is hard for me to use.
It's impossible for her to speak English fluently.

### 2.

It was sweet of you to remember my birthday.
It was careless of him to say that.
It's kind of you to help me.
It was nice of you to e-mail me.
It was stupid of her to do that.
It was rude of you to yell at him

### 3.

I want to go out.
I want you to come on time.

### 4.

It's good to be diligent.
It's not a good idea to skip that class.

---

## Unit 31_ to 부정사를 이용한 다양한 표현

P.128

### Dialogue

A: 나 영어를 잘 못하는 것 같아.
B: 아니야, 네 영어는 대화 나누기에 충분해.
A: 정말 그렇게 생각해?
B: 물론이지. 걱정하지마.

### Unit Test

### 1.

1. To make matters worse  2. Strange to say
3. To tell the truth

### 2.

1. too, to           2. enough, to
3. too, to           4. enough, to
5. too, to           6. enough, to
7. enough, to        8. enough, to

### 3.

1. Her English is good enough to become an English teacher.
2. That coat is too expensive to buy.
3. They are old enough to get married.
4. I was too surprised to say a thing.
5. It's too far to walk there.

## Writing Pattern Practice

### 1.

to make matters worse
To make matters worse, I fell down on my way here.
to tell the truth
To tell the truth, I don't want to sell my house.
strange to say
Strange to say, but I don't want to make much money.

### 2.

I'm too tired to go out.
It's too cold to play soccer outside.
Tim is too young to drive.
That coat is too expensive to buy.
It is too far to walk there.
I was too surprised to say a thing.
The shelf is too high to reach.
This bag is too heavy to carry.

### 3.

You're old enough to see that movie.
Your English is good enough to be understood.
They are old enough to get married.
Sam is rich enough to buy a BMW.
The boy is smart enough to understand this book.
She's tall enough to be a model.

---

## Unit 32_ 동명사의 역할

P.131

### Dialogue

A: 1교시에 왜 늦었어?
B: 늦잠잤어.
A: 그럴 줄 알았어.
B: 매일 일어나는 것은 너무 어려워.

## Unit Test

**1.**
1. 현  2. 동  3. 현  4. 동  5. 동
6. 현  7. 동  8. 현  9. 현  10. 현

**2.**
1. 주  2. 주  3. 목  4. 주  5. 전  6. 목  7. 전

**3.**
1. I don't mind helping you.
2. It started raining.
3. I enjoy visiting other countries.
4. She prefers traveling by car.
5. Eating less is good for your health.
6. It stopped snowing.
7. They kept walking.

## Writing Pattern Practice

**1.**
Exercising every day is good for your health.
Being kind to everyone is not easy.
Getting up early every day is difficult.
It was nice talking to you.
Getting there in an hour is impossible.

**2.**
I like playing soccer.
I hate eating alone.
The car needs repairing.
I enjoy seeing all kinds of movies.
He quit smoking.
Eating less is good for your health.
It started snowing.
It stopped snowing

**3.**
My hobby is watching movies.
My part time job is cooking in a restaurant.
My favorite sport is playing tennis.

**4.**
Thank you for helping me.
I feel like dancing.
I'm used to sleeping on the bus.
I don't mind helping you.
I'm looking forward to seeing you.

---

## Unit 33_ 목적어로 쓰이는 부정사와 동명사

P.134

### Dialogue

A: 뭐가 잘못됐지?
B: 몰라. 울음을 멈추지 않아.
A: 배고픈 것 같은데.
B: 아, 밥 먹이는 걸 잊었다.

### Unit Test

**1.**
1. to drink 2. crying 3. smoking  4. to eat

**2.**
1. exercising          2. going
3. to eat              4. to see
5. moving              6. to study
7. to fly

**3.**
1. F   2. T   3. T   4. F   5. T

**4.**
1. Everybody stopped talking.
2. Don't keep bothering me.
3. I gave up trying to lose weight.
4. I decided not to go out.
5. Don't forget to give me a call.

### Writing Pattern Practice

**1.**
I want to eat pizza.
I decided not to leave for Japan.
I didn't expect to see you here.

**2.**
I finished working.
I don't mind helping you.
I enjoy learning English.

**3.**
I like to watch movies.
= I like watching movies.
I love to cook.
= I love cooking.
I prefer to watch soccer games.
= I prefer watching soccer games.
I hate to be alone.

= I hate being alone.
It started to snow.
= It started snowing.
It began to rain.
= It began raining.
I continued to talk.
= I continued talking.

## 4.
Remember to go to see a doctor today.
I remember seeing him once before.
Don't forget to give me a call.
I forgot about calling you.
I forgot to call you.
I tried eating Mexican food.
I tried to help him.

## REVIEW 1

### 1.
① I want to go out.
② Playing the piano is my hobby.
③ I enjoy sleeping.
④ Jane needs to buy a coat.
⑤ I'm used to taking a shower in the morning.

### 2.
① 나의 목표는 가수가 되는 것이다.
② 너는 그런 일을 하는 것 보니 어리석었다.
③ 이 책은 읽기에 재미있었다.
④ 나는 전에 그를 봤던 것을 기억한다.
⑤ 나는 너에게 전화할 것을 잊었다.

### 3.
① seeing → to see　　② go → to go
③ are → be　　④ read → to read
⑤ talk → talk to(=talk with)
⑥ going → to go
⑦ enough old → old enough
⑧ seeing → to see
⑨ to open → opening
⑩ to work → working

해설
① hope은 to 부정사를 목적어로 취한다.
② want는 to 부정사를 목적어로 취한다.
③ to부정사는 「to+동사원형」이다.
④ '읽을 책' 은 'a book to read' 이다.
⑤ '말할 사람' 은 'someone to talk to(=with)' 이다.
⑥ 「too ~ to ...」는 '너무 ~ 해서 ... 할 수 없다' 는

뜻이다.
⑦ 「형용사+enough」 어순임을 유의한다.
⑧ expect는 to 부정사를 목적어로 취한다.
⑨ mind는 동명사를 목적어로 취한다.
⑩ finish는 동명사를 목적어로 취한다.

### 4.
① to see　　② to exercise
③ working　　④ gambling
⑤ to study　　⑥ eating
⑦ changing　　⑧ to leave
⑨ to go　　⑩ wearing

## REVIEW 2

1. ①　2. ③　3. ③　4. ⑤　5. ②
6. ④　7. ⑤　8. ④　9. ①

해설
1. 보기의 to 부정사는 부사역할을 한다. ②-형용사역
할, ③-명사역할, ④-명사역할, ⑤-형용사역할
2. 보기의 동명사는 목적어역할을 한다. ①-주어역할,
②-전치사의 목적어역할, ④-주어역할, ⑤-전치사
의 목적어역할.
3. ①-feel like~ing, ②-be used to~ing, ④-~nice
talking, ⑤-~is to be~.
4. 의미상의 주어 앞에 전치사 of를 쓸 때는 형용사가
사람의 성질을 나타내는 경우이다.
5. 주어자리이므로 주어자리에 들어갈 수 있는 명사,
동명사, 대명사 중에 하나를 선택해야한다.
6. '밖에 너무 추워서 축구를 할 수 없다' 라는 뜻이므
로 「too~to~」구문을 이용한다.
7. ⑤번은 주어역할이고 나머지는 형용사역할을 한다.
8. ④번은 부사역할이고 ①, ③번은 목적어자리에서
명사역할, ②번은 주어자리에서 명사역할, ⑤번은
형용사역할을 한다.
9. 각각 형용사, 부사역할을 하는 to 부정사의 to가 필
요하다.

해석
사람들은 보드게임을 매우 좋아한다. 왜냐하면 재미있
기 때문이다. 어떤 게임은 짧고 어떤 게임은 하루 종일
걸린다.
우리는 두명 또는 가끔 여덟 명 까지 게임을 할 수 있
다. 많은 종류의 보드 게임이 있다. 우리는 말을 옮기
기 위해서 카드를 뽑거나 주사위를 던진다. 이기거나
지거나 매우 재미있다. 미국에서 가장 인기 있는 보드
게임 중의 하나는 모노폴리이다. 그것은 한국의 부루
마블과 유사하다.

# Chapter 07 | 분사

## Unit 34_ 현재분사

P.140

### Dialogue

A: 유모차에 앉아 있는 아기를 봐.
B: 정말 귀엽다!
A: 우리를 보고 웃고 있어.
B: 응, 그러네. 웃는 모습이 예쁘다.

### Unit Test

**1.**
1. crying  2. dancing  3. watching

**2.**
1. child  2. woman  3. baby  4. concert  5. man

**3.**
1. 주격보어            2. 목적격보어
3. 목적격보어          4. 목적격보어
5. 주격보어

**4.**
1. My work is tiring.
2. The man sitting on the bench is Ted.
3. Do you know the woman sitting on the stage?

### Writing Pattern Practice

**1.**
the smiling baby
Look at the smiling baby.
a boring movie
I saw a boring movie last night.
an interesting person
My sister is an interesting person.
a boring concert
It was a boring concert.

**2.**
the man smiling over there
Look at the man smiling over there.
the girl playing the piano
The girl playing the piano is my daughter.
the man sitting on the bench
Do you know the man sitting on the bench?
the man standing over there
The man standing over there is my boyfriend.

**3.**
I'm taking a shower.
I'm feeding the dog.
You're studying hard.
My father is washing his car.
We're having a party.
The movie seems interesting.

**4.**
I saw you walking with Kate.
I saw John cheating.
I heard a baby crying last night.
Did you hear them fighting?
I kept you waiting.

## Unit 35_ 과거분사

P.143

### Dialogue

A: 그동안 어떻게 지냈어?
B: 일하느라 바빴지.
A: 새로운 일은 어때?
B: 좋아. 정말 만족해.

### Unit Test

**1.**
1. broken  2. fallen  3. interested

**2.**
1. leaves  2. cars  3. university  4. song  5. book

**3.**
1. 주격보어            2. 주격보어
3. 목적격보어          4. 주격보어
5. 목적격보어

**4.**
1. Look at the parked cars.
2. He looked satisfied with his new job.
3. Hotels have rooms filled with sheets and towels.

### Writing Pattern Practice

**1.**
a used car
Eric bought a used car.
fallen leaves
There are some fallen leaves on the ground.
the broken door

Look at the broken door.

## 2.

the cars parked on the street
Look at the cars parked on the street.
one of the languages spoken in many countries
English is  one of the languages spoken in many countries.
the university attended by Britney Spears
This is the university attended by Britney Spears.
a book written by O'Henry
I bought a book written by O'Henry.

## 3.

I'm tired.
I'm bored.
I'm embarrassed.
I'm excited.
I'm interested.
I'm confused.
I'm disappointed.
I'm surprised.
I'm shocked.
I'm satisfied.
I'm depressed.

## 4.

I found the store closed.
I want my shoes repaired.
I heard my name called.

## Unit 36_ 분사구문

| P.146

### Dialogue

A: 지난 밤에 어디 갔었어? 여러 번 전화했는데.
B: 자고 있었어. 피곤해서 일찍 잠자리에 들었어.

### Unit Test

### 1.

1. Shocked  2. Turning  3. Not having  4. Tired
5. doing  6. Working  7. Watching  8. Putting on
9. Not knowing  10. Written

### 2.

1. Talking to you  2. Having ho time
3. Going straight  4.Waving his hand

### 3.

1. Singing  2. Not having  3. Excited

## Writing Pattern Practice

### 1.

Seeing me, he ran away.
Hearing the news, I was surprised.
Going into my room, I turned on the TV.
Having no time, I hurried up.

### 2.

Turning right, you'll see a bank.
Listening to music, you should not study.
Chewing gum, he kept talking.

### 3.

Not having lunch, I was hungry.
Not having a car, she walked here.

### 4.

(Being) tired at work, I came home early.
Written in French, I can't read that book.

## REVIEW I

### 1.

① girl playing the piano
② cars parked on the street
③ man playing soccer in the field
④ man sitting on the bench
⑤ woman standing (over) there

### 2.

① 나는 그가 춤추고 있는 것을 봤다.
② 나는 아기가 울고 있는 것을 들었다.
③ 나는 너를 계속 기다리게 했다.
④ 나는 서가에 소설책들이 가득 차 있는 것을 발견했다.
⑤ 밝게 웃으며 그는 내게 걸어왔다.

### 3.

① walked → walking    ② watch → watching
③ excited → exciting   ④ take → taking
⑤ bored → boring
⑥ interesting → interested
⑦ pleasing → pleased
⑧ Eaten → Eating
⑨ Knowing not→ Not knowing
⑩ Finished → Finishing

① 「지각동사 see+목적어+동사/동사-ing」
② 「지각동사 watch+목적어+동사/동사-ing」
③ excite는 '신나게 하다' 뜻으로 '그 이야기가 신나게 한다' 라고 써야한다.
④ 현재 진행형 문장으로 현재분사를 써야한다.
⑤ bore는 '지루하게 하다' 뜻으로 '그 영화가 지루하게 했다' 라고 써야한다.
⑥ interest는 '흥미를 느끼게 하다' 뜻으로 주어의 느낌을 말할 때는 「be동사+과거분사」형태로 써야한다.
⑦ please는 '내가 기쁘다' 라고 할 때는 be pleased의 형태를 쓴다.
⑧ As I ate too much, I couldn't eat another bite. 라는 문장을 분사구문을 포함한 문장으로 바꾼 것이다. 접속사와 주어를 생략하고 동사에 ~ing를 붙이면 Eating too much, ~라고 써야 한다.
⑨ 분사구문의 부정은 분사 앞에 not을 붙인다.
⑩ After she finished her homework, she went to bed.이라는 문장을 분사구문을 포함한 문장으로 바꾼 것이다. 접속사와 주어를 생략하고 동사에 ~ing를 붙이면 Finishing her homework, ~라고 써야 한다.

**4.**

① shocking
② boring
③ embarrassed
④ exciting
⑤ depressing
⑥ interested
⑦ disappointed
⑧ Being mean
⑨ Not feeling
⑩ Listening

**REVIEW 2**

1. ⑤  2. ⑤  3. ①  4. ③  5. ①  6. ④  7. ④

1. ⑤번은 목적격보어로 쓰인 현재분사이고 나머지는 명사를 꾸며주는 현재분사이다.
2. ⑤번은 현재완료 문장에 쓰인 과거분사고 나머지는 명사를 꾸며주는 과거분사다.
3. ② bored→boring  ③ Eaten→Eating
   ④ interested→interesting
   ⑤ Knowing not→Not knowing
4. '내차가 온통 움푹 들어갔다. 나는 그것이 고쳐졌으면 좋겠다' 라는 문장이다. dent는 '움푹 들어가게 하다' 라는 뜻으로 '움푹 들어갔다' 라고 하려면 be dented를 써야한다. 그리고 목적어 it과 repair와의 관계가 '수리당하다' 라는 수동관계이므로

repaired를 써야한다.
5. ①번은 과거형이고 나머지는 과거분사로 쓰였다.
6. 그녀는 멀리 살아서 크리스마스에 거의 못 온다.
7. Isn't it surprising?(surprise:놀랍게하다, 놀랍지 않나요?) You must be interested.(interest: 흥미를 주다, 너는 흥미가 있음에 틀림없다.)

당신은 육지에서 가장 무거운 동물이 무엇인지 아십니까? 그것은 코끼리입니다. 바다에서 가장 무거운 동물은요? 그것은 바다표범입니다. 숫 바다표범은 4000 kg까지 무게가 나갑니다. 그것은 차의 두배 무게죠. 놀랍지 않습니까? 당신은 그것들이 무엇을 먹는지에 흥미로워 할 것임에 틀림없습니다. 이상하게도 그들은 큰 것들을 먹지는 않습니다. 그들은 낙지, 오징어, 그리고 홍합을 먹습니다. 그들은 자주 한끼로 그것들을 많이 먹습니다.

# Chapter 08 | 수동태

## Unit 37_ 능동태와 수동태

| P.152

### Dialogue

A: 뭐야?
B: 몰라. 일본말로 쓰여 있어.
A: 어디보자. 너 Akiko 생일파티에 초대 되었어.
B: 정말? 그거 좋은데.

### Unit Test

**1.**
1. Ellis is loved by everybody.
2. Frogs are eaten by snakes.
3. I was bitten by a mosquito.
4. This cake was made by my mother.
5. I was used by my boss.

**2.**
1. Is Jinny loved by everyone?
2. Jinny was loved by everyone.
3. Jinny will be loved by everyone.
4. Jinny has been loved by everyone.

**3.**
1. is spoken
2. are imported
3. was invited
4. was stolen

5. was made

**4.**

1. That building was built 100 years ago.
2. When were you born?
3. This cake was made for Michael.

## Writing Pattern Practice

**1.**

Jane is loved by everybody.
I was bitten by a mosquito.
This cake was made by my mother.

**2.**

English is spoken in many countries.
The window is broken.
The letter was written in Chinese.
I was born in Seoul.
Rome wasn't built in a day.

**3.**

I'm helped by many people.
You aren't allowed to park here.

**4.**

When were you born?
This house was built 10 years ago.

**5.**

You will be punished.
The store will be closed at 9 pm.
The meeting will be held this Friday.

**6.**

Dinner is being made.
The bread is being baked.
The car is being towed away.

**7.**

The secret has been kept for a long time.
The Pizza has been delivered.

## Unit 38_ 수동태표현

| P.155

## Dialogue

A(엄마): 뭔가 냄새 좋은데.
B: Mary가 케익 만들고 있어요. 파티에 가져간대요.
A: 너도 파티에 초대 받았니?
B: 네. 정말 기대되요.

## Unit Test

**1.**

1. John was run over by a truck
2. My baby should be taken care of by me.
3. The pizza can be delivered by them.
4. This work may be done by me.
5. The baggage was picked up by a man.

**2.**

1. That song is liked by young people.
2. The letter wasn't written in English.
3. This room isn't cleaned everyday.
4. Was she surprised at the news?
5. Are people interested in movies?

**3.**

1. to  2. in  3. with  4. with  5. at(by)

**4.**

1. Many stars can be seen in this weather.
2. When was the car towed away?
3. The problem can't be solved.

## Writing Pattern Practice

**1.**

That movie is not liked by young people.
The letter wasn't written in English.
It was not made in Italy.
The problem has not been solved.

**2.**

Was it painted by Picasso?
Will the thief be caught soon?
Where was the child found?
When was that book published?

**3.**

Jane was run over by a truck.
David was laughed at by his classmates.
The baby is being taken care of a baby-sitter.

**4.**

This work can be done right away.
The car may be parked over there.

**5.**

The mountain is covered with snow.
I'm interested in sports.
Are you satisfied with your job?
I was surprised at/by the news.

All of us are pleased with the result.

## REVIEW 1

**1.**
① The store was closed at 6.
② That song is loved by young people.
③ The book will be published soon.
④ I was bitten by a mosquito.
⑤ Mangos are not grown in Korea.

**2.**
① 나는 파티에 절대 초대받지 못한다.
② 그 문제는 해결될 수 있다.
③ 너는 음악에 관심 있니?
④ 그것은 미국에서 만든 것이니?
⑤ 그 아기는 베이비시터에 의해 보살핌을 받고 있다.

**3.**
① born → was born ② spoken → is spoken
③ grow → grown ④ cancel → canceled
⑤ catch → caught ⑥ a car → by a car
⑦ speak→spoken ⑧ love → loved
⑨ write → written ⑩ visit → visited

**해설**
① '나는 홍콩에서 태어났다.' 라는 수동태문장으로 I 와 born 사이에 was를 써야한다.
② '중국에는 무슨 언어가 쓰이는가?' 라는 수동태문장으로 language와 spoken 사이에 is를 써야한다.
③ '오렌지가 한국에서 재배되는가?' 라는 수동태문장으로 grow대신 grown을 써야한다.
④ '그 회의가 취소되었다.' 라는 수동태 문장으로 cancel 대신 canceled를 써야한다.
⑤ '도둑이 잡히지 않았다.' 라는 수동태 문장으로 catch 대신 caught을 써야한다.
⑥ 'John이 차에 치었다.' 라는 수동태 문장으로 a car 앞에 by가 필요하다.
⑦ '멕시코에서는 스페인어가 사용되는가?' 라는 수동태 문장으로 speak대신 spoken을 써야한다.
⑧ '매운 음식은 태국에서 사랑받는다.' 라는 수동태 문장으로 love대신 loved를 써야한다.
⑨ 'Harry Potter는 Joan K. Rolling에 의해 쓰여졌다.' 라는 수동태 문장으로 write대신 written을 써야한다.
⑩ '디즈니랜드는 많은 사람들에 의해 방문되어져 왔다.' 라는 수동태문장으로 visit 대신 visited를 써야한다.

**4.**
① in ② by ③ for ④ by ⑤ in
⑥ at ⑦ with ⑧ in ⑨ by ⑩ by

## REVIEW 2

1. ② 2. ① 3. ⑤ 4. ② 5. ② 6. ②
7. ③ 8. ②

**해설**
1. be satisfied with '~에 만족하다'
   be covered with '~로 덮여있다'
   be pleased with '~에 만족하다, 기뻐하다'
2. ② speak → spoken ③ build → built
   ④ fire → fired ⑤ cook → cooked
3. ⑤번 문장은 '다이아몬드반지가 발견되지 않았다' 라는 수동태문장으로 find 대신 found를 써야한다.
4. '야구는 대부분의 나라에서 행해진다.' 라는 수동태 문장으로 빈칸에 is played를 써야한다.
5. '이 단어가 어떻게 발음 되는지 아니?' 라는 수동태 문장으로 빈칸에 is pronounced를 써야한다.
6. '어디에서 태어났니?' 는 'Where were you born?' 으로 수동태문장을 쓴다.
7. '많은 사람들이 사고에서 부상을 당했다' 라는 수동태 문장으로 빈칸에 were injured를 써야한다.
8. '~로 가득 차다' 는 'be filled with' 를, '~를 검사 받다' 는 '~be checked' 를 쓴다.

**해석**
우리는 비행기를 타기위해 공항에 간다. 공항은 서로 다른 나라에서 온 비행기들로 가득 차 있다. 어떤 것은 이륙하기를 기다리고 어떤 것은 착륙을 기다리고 있다. 비행기가 착륙할 때는 안전을 위해 조심스럽게 검사 받는다. 타이어와 엔진을 검사받는다. 연료도 다시 채워진다. 모든 것이 검사되면 새로운 탑승객이 (비행기에) 오른다.

# BASIC
# English
# Grammar
*for Speaking & Writing*